Commission on Nursing

Interim Report

October 1997

BAILE ÁTHA CLIATH
ARNA FHOILSIÚ AG OIFIG AN tSOLÁTHAIR
Le ceannach díreach ón
OIFIG DHÍOLTA FOILSEACHÁN RIALTAIS, TEACH SUN ALLIANCE,
SRÁID THEACH LAIGHEAN, BAILE ÁTHA CLIATH 2,
nó tríd an bpost ó
FOILSEACHÁIN RIALTAIS, AN RANNÓG POST-TRÁCHTA,
4 - 5 BÓTHAR FHEARCHAIR, BAILE ÁTHA CLIATH 2,
(Teil: 01 - 6613111 — fo-líne 4040/4045; Fax: 01 - 4752760)
nó trí aon díoltóir leabhar.

DUBLIN
PUBLISHED BY THE STATIONERY OFFICE
To be purchased directly from the
GOVERNMENT PUBLICATIONS SALE OFFICE, SUN ALLIANCE HOUSE,
MOLESWORTH STREET, DUBLIN 2,
or by mail order from
GOVERNMENT PUBLICATIONS, POSTAL TRADE SECTION,
4 - 5 HARCOURT ROAD, DUBLIN 2,
(Tel: 01 - 6613111 — ext. 4040/4045; Fax: 01 - 4752760)
or through any bookseller.

£2.50

Wt. 50695. 10/97. 5,000. Cahill. (M25532). G.Spl.

Table of Contents

Chapter 3

Preparation for the Profession

Chapter 4

Professional Development

Chapter 5

Regulation of the Nursing Profession

Chapter 6

The Role of Nurses in the Management of Services

Chapter 7

The Employment Conditions of Nurses

CHAPTER 1

Introduction and Brief Overview of Nursing in Ireland

Content of the Interim report

1.1 The Interim Report reflects the initial phase of the work of the Commission. This phase concentrated on an identification of the issues as articulated by the nursing profession and others. The Commission through the consultative process sought to determine the issues of concern to interested parties, primarily nurses of all disciplines, within its terms of reference. The Interim Report identifies the issues put forward by those attending the consultative fora and in written submissions. The Commission has not as yet reached any conclusions in relation to the issues identified in this phase of its deliberations. The issues identified are complex and many are inter-related and some reflect broader issues within the health and public sector in general. Many of the issues identified reflect the increasingly diverse and complex nature of nursing services in this country. The Commission now intends to consider these issues in its deliberations and will address them in the final report, within the context of its terms of reference.

Terms of Reference and Membership of Commission

1.2 The Commission on Nursing was established following a recommendation from the Labour Court (Recommendation No. LCR15450) in March, 1997. The Labour Court, in its deliberations on a series of issues in dispute between health service employers and the Alliance of Nursing Unions, recognised that there had been extensive changes in the requirements placed on nurses, both in training and the delivery of services. The Labour Court recommended that both parties be involved in agreeing the terms of reference which would be wide ranging and include addressing such items as structural and work changes, segmentation of the grade, training and education requirements, promotional opportunities and related difficulties and a general assessment of the evolving role of nurses.

1.3 The Commission was established by the Minister for Health on 21 March, 1997. The agreed terms of reference were as follows:

The Commission will examine and report on the role of nurses in the health service including:

- **the evolving role of nurses, reflecting their professional development and their role in the overall management of services;**

- **promotional opportunities and related difficulties;**

- **structural and work changes appropriate for the effective and efficient discharge of that role;**

- **the requirements placed on nurses, both in training and the delivery of services;**

- **segmentation of the grade; and**

- **training and education requirements.**

In its recommendations it should seek to provide a secure basis for the further professional development of nursing in the context of anticipated changes in health services, their organisation and delivery.

1.4 In the light of discussions during the consultative process undertaken by the Commission, which are detailed below, and following the agreement of An Bord Altranais, the Commission wrote to the Minister for Health on 1 August, 1997 seeking an extension of its terms of reference to include:

> **the role and function of An Bord Altranais generally, including, inter alia, education and professional development, regulation and protection of the citizen.**

1.5 The Minister for Health agreed to this extension of the terms of reference of the Commission on 12 September, 1997. An Bord Altranais has not as yet had an opportunity to make submissions on the revised terms of reference.

1.6 The Minister for Health appointed the following persons to be members of the Commission:

Chair:
Ms. Justice Mella Carroll

Members:
Dr. Ruth Barrington, Assistant Secretary, Department of Health

Mr. Leslie Buckley, Management Consultant

Ms. Kay Collins, Staff Nurse, University College Hospital, Galway

Mr. Denis Doherty, Chief Executive Officer, Midland Health Board

Ms. Antoinette Doocey, Public Health Nurse, North-Eastern Health Board

Ms. Sandra Guilfoyle, Personnel Consultant

Mr. Philip Halpin, Chief Operating Officer, National Irish Bank

Ms. Eilish Hardiman, Ward Sister, St. James's Hospital

Mr. Des Kavanagh, General Secretary, Psychiatric Nurses Association

Mr. P.J. Madden, General Secretary, Irish Nurses Organisation

Dr. Geraldine McCarthy-Haslam, Department of Nursing, University College, Cork

Dr. David McCutcheon, Chief Executive Officer, Tallaght Hospital

Mr. Leo O'Donnell, Chartered Accountant

Ms. Peta Taaffe, Director of Nursing, St. James's Hospital

1.7 Dr. David McCutcheon resigned from the Commission on 23 May, 1997 because of an increased workload associated with revised plans for the opening of the hospital in Tallaght.

Consultative Process

1.8 The Commission organised a series of consultative fora throughout the country to hear the views of nurses and other health professionals on the range of issues within the terms of reference of the Commission. Each forum consisted of three sessions from 9.30 a.m. to 12.30 p.m., 2.00 p.m. to 5.00 p.m. and 6.30 p.m. to 9.30 p.m. respectively. Participants were invited to attend the session of their choice and entrance was by ticket only, issued on a first come, first served basis. The sessions were organised on a workshop basis, with each workshop choosing its own chair and rapporteur. Those attending a session were randomly assigned to a workshop to ensure a spread of nursing disciplines in every workshop. An exception was made for nurse managers, those above ward sister level, who were assigned to a workshop together. This was on the basis of experience at an early consultative forum, where the presence of nurse management and staff nurses from the same hospital in the same workshop appeared to constrain a full and frank discussion.

1.9 At least one member of the Commission sat in on each workshop to listen to the issues raised and discussed. Members of the Commission attending workshops did not actively participate in discussions at workshops but occasionally sought or provided clarification on issues raised. The rapporteur from each workshop reported back to the plenary session on the discussion in a workshop.

Consultative fora were organised, with substantial assistance from the health boards, at the following venues:

10 May, 1997   Tullamore — Midland Health Board

26 May, 1997   Tralee — Southern Health Board

27 May, 1997   Cork — Southern Health Board

29 May, 1997   Limerick — Mid-Western Health Board

30 May, 1997   Galway — Western Health Board

3 June, 1997   Castlebar — Western Health Board

4 June, 1997   Bundoran — North Western Health Board

5 June, 1997   Monaghan — North Eastern Health Board

9 June, 1997   Kilkenny — South Eastern Health Board

10 June, 1997   Waterford — South Eastern Health Board

12 June, 1997   Dublin — Eastern Health Board

13 June, 1997   Maynooth — Eastern Health Board

14 June, 1997   Dublin — Eastern Health Board

1.10 Approximately 3,000 people attended the consultative fora between 10th May and 14th June, 1997. The vast majority were nurses with a small number of other professionals such as pharmacists, career guidance teachers and occupational therapists. All nursing disciplines were represented at the fora.

1.11 In advance of each forum, questions were circulated for consideration at each workshop. This was to enable those attending to have a focused consultation in advance with colleagues who could not attend. It was a matter for each workshop whether the questions were used as a focus for discussion or whether the workshop chose its own agenda entirely. The questions circulated were:

(1) What do you consider is the core role of nursing?

(2) Are there tasks which nurses are asked to perform which you consider are outside this core role?

(3) Are there other activities which you consider appropriate for nurses from which they are excluded?

(4) What are the main difficulties both professional and administrative which hinder nurses from doing a better job?

(5) How can the professional relationship between medical staff and nursing staff be improved?

(6) How do you see the future development of the nursing profession and what career pattern do you envisage for nurses in the next 5-10 years?

(7) What is the most important recommendation you think the Commission could make?

Many workshops addressed and discussed each question in turn; others focused only on a couple of the questions. A small number chose to have a general discussion on nursing issues. However, the questions circulated by the Commission encompassed the broad themes of the discussion in all workshops.

1.12 The Commission placed advertisements in national and provincial newspapers inviting written submissions from interested parties on issues within its terms of reference. Written submissions, totalling 704, were received and these are listed in the appendix to the report. The submissions, from a range of individuals, groups and national bodies, provided an essential resource to the Commission in the identification of issues for consideration within its terms of reference. These submissions will also be used as a resource by the Commission in its deliberations prior to the publication of the final report.

1.13 The Commission invited a number of persons to meet with it to discuss issues within its terms of reference. These were:

Mr. Tom Beegan, Programme Manager, South-Eastern Health Board

Ms. Cecily Begley, Department of Nursing, Trinity College, Dublin 2

Dr. Michael Boland, General Practitioner, Irish College of General Practitioners

Mr. Brendan Byrne, Chief Nursing Officer, St. Dympna's Hospital, Carlow

Ms. Jean Clarke, Lecturer, Co-ordinator Higher Diploma in Nursing Studies (Public Health Nursing), U.C.D.

Ms. Maeve Dwyer, Matron, National Maternity Hospital, Holles St., Dublin

Ms. Helen Flint, Director of Nursing Research and Development, Eastern Health Board

Ms. Christine Hancock, General Secretary, Royal College of Nursing, London

Ms. Joan McDermott, Matron, D'Alton Home, Claremorris, Co. Mayo

Ms. Marie McInerney, Principal Midwifery Tutor, Regional Maternity Hospital, Limerick

Ms. Wilma McPherson, Director of Quality and Nursing, Guys and St. Thomas Hospital, London

Ms. Gertie Monagle, Matron, Carndonagh Community Hospital, Co. Donegal

Ms. Deirdre Seery, Matron, Cottage Hospital, Drogheda, Co. Louth

In addition, the Commission met with the Chief Executive Officers Group of the health boards, a group of directors of nursing and representatives of An Bord Altranais; the Irish Matrons Association, the Irish Medical Council, the Royal College of Surgeons in Ireland, the Royal College of Physicians of Ireland, the Irish College of General Practitioners, and the Irish Medical Organisation.

Next Steps

1.14 The Commission intends to hold three seminars in November, 1997. Representatives of those who made written submissions to the Commission will be invited to attend and discuss the Interim Report and to identify possible solutions to the issues raised. The Commission intends to continue to hold meetings with nurses and other relevant bodies.

1.15 Reviews of literature have already been commissioned in the following areas:

    (i) to identify changes in the professional role of nurses in Ireland; to identify the main social, demographic, legislative, educational and technological developments in Ireland which have impacted on the professional role of nurses in the last seventeen years;

   (ii) to identify the changes, if any, that have taken place internationally on the professional role of nurses which would be of relevance to the professional development of nurses in Ireland. To examine, in particular, any changes that have recently taken place in the United Kingdom. To critically analyse changes which have taken place in other countries and suggest examples of good practice;

  (iii) to examine the role of nurses in the management of health services both in Ireland and internationally. In reviewing literature on international developments to concentrate on developments in the United Kingdom, Europe, North America and Australia/New Zealand, which are of relevance to the role of nurses in the management of the health services in Ireland.

The Central Statistics Office has agreed to include a module on attitudes of the public to nursing services in its Household Survey from September to December, 1997. The results of the survey and literature reviews should prove a valuable resource not only to the Commission but to the nursing profession in general.

The Commission hopes to issue its Final Report towards the middle of 1998.

Brief Overview of Nursing in Ireland

1.16 Nursing is a profession regulated by An Bord Altranais (the Nursing Board) under the Nurses Act 1985. The Board maintains a register, which is divided into seven divisions, namely; general, psychiatric, mental handicap, paediatric, midwifery, public health and tutors. Other smaller divisions and supplementary divisions of the register have been discontinued over time. At the end of 1996 there was a total of 53,641 nurses recorded on the register. Of these 44,822 had paid the annual retention fee for 1996 and were eligible to practice in this country. The Board also maintains an inactive file on the register for nurses who have indicated they do not intend to practice here for the time being. Of the total number registered at the end of 1996, ninety-three percent were women. Nurses may be registered on each division of the register for which they have the appropriate qualification. Qualifications registered on the active file in respect of each division of the register at the end of 1996 were as follows:

Division	Number of Nurses with Qualification
General	36,243
Psychiatric	8,615
Sick Childrens	2,821
Mental Handicap	2,865
Midwifery	12,136
Public Health	1,667
Tutor	331
Other	438
Total	**65,116**

1.17   General nurses usually work in acute hospitals, care of the elderly settings and in general practices. Psychiatric nurses are usually employed in psychiatric hospitals, psychiatric units within acute hospitals, community health centres and in the community. Sick children's nurses usually work in children's hospitals and paediatric units in acute hospitals. Mental handicap nurses are usually employed in residences for people with mental handicap and in some psychiatric hospitals, caring for those with a mental handicap. Midwives usually work in maternity hospitals, maternity units in acute hospitals and in the community. Public health nurses generally work in the community. Nurse tutors are employed in schools of nursing within hospitals or colleges/universities. Nurses may also work in various other settings such as in industry as occupational health nurses.

1.18 The number of nurses employed by health boards and voluntary hospitals/agencies funded directly by the Department of Health at the end of December 1996 totalled 27,264. Of this number 65% were at staff nurse grade. A further breakdown of these figures by employer shows:

Total number of nurses employed by health boards	17,234
Total number of nurses employed by voluntary hospitals	7,886
Total number of nurses in voluntary mental handicap agencies	2,144
Total	27,264*

*This figure excludes nurses employed by voluntary health agencies funded by health boards. Many nurses are employed in private hospitals, nursing homes and by nursing agencies. Others work as practice nurses with general practitioners. Some have chosen to work in the industrial/corporate sector while others have chosen to leave nursing altogether. Significant numbers of Irish nurses work overseas and have made a substantial contribution to the development of health services worldwide.

CHAPTER 2

The Role of the Nurse

The Role of the Nurse

2.1 A common theme running through many submissions made by nurses and discussed at the consultative fora organised by the Commission was concern in relation to the varying perceptions of the role of the nurse. Whilst there appeared to be general agreement in relation to a theoretical concept of the core role of nursing, it seemed that many nurses believed their actual role in the daily delivery of health services was undervalued and under recognised. Other professionals within the health services such as medical practitioners and paramedical staff, it was argued, had more clearly defined roles and staff responsibilities. The clear parameters within which these professionals appeared to operate was perceived as allowing for a greater understanding of roles within a multi-disciplinary team and contributing to better working relationships. Nurses considered that their role was poorly defined and understood and this made it difficult for nurses to contribute to their full potential within a multi-disciplinary team. It was suggested that other professionals may not fully appreciate what nurses can contribute towards the achievement of particular goals. Some nurses argued that they were perceived by many within the health services as those who carried out the tasks that no other group performed and who filled gaps in the service rather than as professionals with a particular role, function and contribution. This chapter seeks to identify some of the concerns of nurses in general in relation to their role and to identify the particular concerns of certain disciplines in relation to their role.

The Core Role of Nursing

2.2 The Commission on Nursing requested those attending workshops at the consultative fora organised by the Commission to consider the question — what is the core role of nursing? Nearly all participants at workshops stated that the core role of the nurse involved caring and was patient centred. Many workshops in responding to this question, whilst acknowledging the difficulty in defining the core role of nursing, gave the definition of nursing proposed by Virginia Henderson (1960),which states:

> *"The unique function of the nurse is to assist the individual, sick or well, in the performance of those activities contributing to health or its recovery (or to a peaceful death) that he would perform unaided had he the necessary strength, will or knowledge, and to do so in such a way as to help him gain independence as rapidly as possible. . . ."*

2.3 A good description of the core role of nursing was given in a workshop in Monaghan in the North-Eastern health board, which was:

> *"the role of the nurse is based on the nursing process which involves identifying patients needs, devising a plan of appropriate care, implementing that plan with follow-up evaluation. Nurses have a role to play in health promotion, education of patients, relatives and staff. The specific role that nurses have varies with the particular area that they work in, be it acute hospital services, geriatric, psychiatric, mental handicap or public health. However nurses are at all times the patient's advocate and must maintain and deliver high standards of care to patients. Nurses take a holistic approach and work as part of a multi-disciplinary team."*

2.4 The definition of nursing approved by the International Council of Nurses in 1978 was also referred to the Commission. This states:

> *"Nursing encompasses the promotion of health, prevention of illness and care of physically ill, mentally ill, and disabled people of all ages, in all health care and other community settings.... the phenomenon of particular concern to nurses is individual, family and group responses to actual or potential health problems. The unique function of nurses in caring for individuals, sick or well, is to assess their responses to their health status and to assist them in the performance of those activities contributing to health, recovery, or to dignified death, that*

they would perform unaided if they had the necessary strength, will or knowledge to do this in such a way as to help them gain full or partial independence as rapidly as possible."

2.5 It appeared from the discussions at the workshops and from the written submissions received by the Commission that nurses from all disciplines, despite the disparate settings in which nursing care was provided, retained a sense of professional unity relating to the core role of nursing.

2.6 However, a number of midwives, in their submissions relating to the core role of nursing, suggested that midwifery should be recognised as a profession distinct from nursing in this country. The concerns of midwives will be dealt with later in this chapter.

Tasks Outside The Core Role Of Nursing

2.7 Whilst nurses appeared to agree on the principles of their core role, there seemed to be some concern in relation to the variety of tasks nurses were asked to perform on a daily basis. Nurses were of the view that there were many tasks, such as portering, clerical work or domestic tasks such as washing and making empty beds, being performed by nurses which were outside their core nursing role. A great variety of tasks currently performed by nurses were identified as being non-nursing duties and the examples given are purely illustrative; it would not be within the remit of this report to attempt to give an exhaustive list. In general, nurses perceived that if an action involved a therapeutic intervention then it was a nursing action. Whether or not a particular interaction involved a therapeutic intervention with patients gave rise to much interesting debate and nurses gave many different perspectives on the matter.

2.8 The frequency with which non-nursing tasks were being performed by nurses appeared to be impacting on the morale and sense of professionalism of nurses. There was a view that if no other person in a health care setting would perform a particular task that a nurse was expected to take responsibility for doing it. The opinion was offered that the use of nurses for non-professional, non-therapeutic duties did not make optimal use of highly trained and skilled professional health care workers and was not cost-effective.

2.9   The relationship of nurses to non-nursing support staff (referred to hereafter as non-nursing personnel) gave rise to much discussion at the consultative fora and in written submissions. There seemed to be a general acceptance amongst nurses that there was a need for the greater use of non-nursing personnel. Some nurses expressed concern that the use of such workers was driven by a desire to find cheap alternatives to nurses and that their greater use would result in the recruitment of fewer nurses with a consequential impact on the quality of care provided by the health services. Concern was also expressed that there was currently a lack of standardisation between hospitals in relation to the recruitment criteria, training provided to and titles of non-nursing personnel. It was suggested that the relationship of such workers to nurses would require careful consideration and that attention needed to be given to the roles and responsibilities of such staff vis-à-vis nurses.

Midwifery

2.10   It was argued by some midwives that the Nurses Act 1985, which governs the regulation of the nursing profession, fails to recognise the separate and unique role of midwives by defining a nurse as also including a midwife. It was argued that midwives had a distinct role in the delivery of care to well women during the course of a normal pregnancy. Many European countries offer direct entry into midwifery and midwifery students are not registered general nurses in those countries. Midwifery training and practice are dealt with under a separate EU Directive, 80/155/EEC.

2.11   The definition of a midwife adopted by the International Confederation of Midwives (ICM) and the International Federation of Gynaecologists and Obstetricians (FIGO), in 1972 and 1973 respectively and later adopted by the World Health Organisation (WHO) was given in a number of submissions to the Commission. The definition was amended by the ICM in 1990 and the amendment ratified by the FIGO and the WHO in 1991 and 1992 respectively and now reads:

"A midwife is a person who, having been regularly admitted to a midwifery educational programme, duly recognised in the country in which it is located, has successfully completed the prescribed course of studies in midwifery and has acquired the requisite qualifications to be registered and/or legally licensed to practice midwifery. She must be able to give the necessary supervision, care and advice to

women during pregnancy, labour and postpartum period, to conduct deliveries on her own responsibility and to care for the newborn and the infant. This care includes preventative measures, the detection of abnormal conditions in mother and child, the procurement of medical assistance and the execution of emergency measures in the absence of medical help. She has an important task in health counselling and education, not only for the women, but also within the family and the community. The work should involve antenatal education and preparation for parenthood and extends to certain areas of gynaecology, family planning and child care. She may practice in hospitals, clinics, health units, domiciliary conditions or in any other service."

2.12 Concern was expressed in relation to the current supervisory arrangements for domiciliary midwives providing for homebirths. Health boards are obliged under the Health Act 1970 to provide domiciliary midwifery care for women who wish to give birth at home. It was reported that in 1996, there were 50,390 registered births in Ireland, of which 206 were home births (Source: CSO, 1996 provisional figures). Domiciliary midwives are subject to general supervision and control by the health board in the geographical area in which the birth is taking place. The person designated by health boards to exercise this supervision and control is a superintendent public health nurse. There was concern expressed by superintendent public health nurses and midwives in relation to this arrangement.

2.13 Many midwives expressed the view that midwifery practice had become increasingly constrained in recent years and that midwives were becoming de-skilled in the provision of maternity services. Many midwives suggested that the increasing "medicalisation" of normal pregnancies had turned midwives into obstetric nurses rather than the independent practitioners allowed by their education. It was suggested that midwifery provided substantial scope for the development of a woman centred care service before, during and after pregnancy. In order for midwifery to develop its potential for the delivery of women centred care, it was suggested that the regulatory framework for nursing practice needed to recognise the distinct identity of midwives.

Mental Handicap Nursing

2.14 Services for people with a mental handicap (also referred to as intellectual disability) have evolved in recent years with a greater emphasis on integration at school, work, and in the community. The mental

21

handicap nurse works with all age ranges and all levels of handicap including persons with greater dependency; mild, moderate, severe, profound and multiple handicaps. The age range includes an increasing population of senior citizens. A wide range of services are provided, such as—

- residential and respite care, which is inclusive of community group houses and local centres;

- day care including assessments, early intervention services, pre-school, special education development; and

- vocational training, sheltered and supported employment.

A number of submissions suggested that the role of the mental handicap nurse needed to be clearly defined in an increasingly diverse and complex service for those with such a handicap. There was a need to respond to changes taking place within the service such as the increasing age profile and increasingly complex range of disabilities of those with a mental handicap. Submissions referred to the need for nurses to be at the centre of the service responding to these changing needs and suggested that the skills of the mental handicap nurse needed to be retained and developed to ensure the on-going development of a quality and responsive service. Some mental handicap nurses expressed concern in relation to a lack of appreciation of the specialist skills of mental handicap nurses with the increasing employment of general nurses, teachers and non-nursing personnel in these services.

2.15 The Commission received a copy of the Report of the Working Group on the Role of the Mental Handicap Nurse from the Department of Health and will consider the report in its deliberations.

Sick Children's Nursing

2.16 It was suggested by registered sick children's nurses that nursing children differs from nursing adults because of their special health care needs. It was submitted that children were physically and emotionally different from adults and needed constant care and support from their parents. Children, therefore, required care from specially skilled staff. Because of the age range of patients, sick children's nurses required an in-depth understanding of the physical, psychological, social development and maturation processes from infancy to early adulthood. Sick children's nurses needed acute skills of observation and communication as frequently their patients were not capable of telling them what was wrong with them and might be totally dependent on them. It was submitted that in promoting the concept of family centred care the sick children's nurse required special skills in teaching and support by entering into partnership with families in the provision of care. It was suggested in a number of submissions to the Commission that there was a need to examine the role of the sick children's nurse in the paediatric service and that the special skills of such nurses be recognised and developed to ensure that nursing services continued to respond to the special needs of sick children.

Public Health Nursing

2.17 The Commission received numerous submissions from individual public health nurses (PHNs) and from groups of public health nurses expressing concern in relation to their role in the delivery of community health services. The current PHN service is based on a Department of Health circular in 1966 on the "District Nursing Service".

The circular outlined the objectives of a community based nursing service which were summarised as follows:

> *"Broadly, the aim should be to make public health nurses available to individuals and to families in each area throughout the country. More specifically, the object should be to provide such domiciliary midwifery services as may be necessary, general domiciliary nursing, particularly for the aged, and at least equally important, to attend to the public health care of children, from infancy to the end of the school going period. The nurses should provide health education in the home, and assist local medical practitioners in the care of patients who need nursing care but who do not require treatment in an institution — whether for medical or social reasons. The aim should be to integrate the district nursing service with the general practitioner, hospital, in-patient and out-patient services, so that the nurse will be able to fulfil the important function of an essential member of the community health team and carry out her duties in association with the hospital staff and other doctors in her district."*

The concept outlined in the circular was of an "all-purpose" public health nursing role encompassing a range of preventative and caring functions.

2.18 It was argued that in the years since the Department of Health circular establishing the current public health nursing system was issued that there had been demographic, legislative, social and health service changes which had impacted on the role of the PHN and that there had been no corresponding review of the role of the PHN in response to these changes.

2.19 A number of PHNs considered that they were facing an ever increasing workload and an increasingly complex range of problems such as drug and child abuse. In addition "specialist" nurses such as palliative care nurses had begun to work in the community and recently practice nurses had been employed by general practitioners to provide nursing services attached to their practice. In these circumstances PHNs argued that there was a need to examine the role of the PHN and to retain and develop the particular "community" skills which they had developed over the years and to examine the need for "specialist" skills in the community nursing service in areas such as wound care and stoma care.

2.20 The requirement of a midwifery qualification for nurses applying to do public health nursing was also raised as an issue during the consultative process. It was felt by some that such a qualification may no longer be required because of the changed service demands currently facing PHNs. It was also seen as discouraging male nurses from becoming PHNs because of the very few who hold a midwifery qualification. It was suggested that alternative education modules on maternity care might be incorporated into the Public Health Nurse Higher Diploma programme.

2.21 The Commission received from the Department of Health a copy of a recent report of a working party on a Review of Public Health Nursing which it will consider in its deliberations.

Psychiatric Nursing

2.22 There have been substantial changes in the provision of mental health services in the last thirty years. In the 1960s there were in excess of 27,000 patients resident in mental health institutions in Ireland. The Commission of Enquiry on Mental Illness report in 1966 paved the way for changes in the provision of mental health services. The in-patient population in mental health institutions had dropped to 11,600 by 1984. The document *Planning for the Future* was published in 1984 and brought about further radical changes in the mental health services with a shift away from institutional based treatment to community structures and services, multi-site service provision and adoption of a unit of care approach rather than a bed based approach. An illustration of the extent of change which has taken place in the past fifteen years was given in a submission which gave the example of one institution which had 985 beds in 1985 reducing to 220 beds in 1997. It was submitted that key agents of change during this period were psychiatric nurses.

2.23 A submission from the Chief Nursing Officers of the Psychiatric Services in the Eastern Health Board gave a description of the role of the psychiatric nurse. This was:

"All nursing requires the establishment of a relationship with patients, however, psychiatric nursing is distinguished by the fact that the care that is delivered is contained in the relationship. It is not in the provision of physical acts of care (although they too have their place in psychiatric nursing), but in the building and nurturing of communication and relationship contacts with the patient that care is delivered . . . . . In psychiatric nursing the amount of time spent with the patient and the relationship established is just as important as clinical background. It is in this sense that psychiatric nursing can be described as largely invisible. There is very little technology involved. It involves a large degree of the use of self and is based on a high degree of interpretative skills as opposed to technical skills. These skills are developed within the profession of psychiatric nursing and used in partnership with other professionals . . . . . Psychiatric nursing requires the skills of interpersonal relationship formation coupled with knowledge of mental health/illness and the adaptation of nursing interactions to ensure a skilled approach to care. In order to fulfil this task, the psychiatric nurse must be able to look after all of the physical needs of patients, understand psychological and social functioning and have a sound knowledge base on which to base the provision of psychiatric nursing care. This entails the ability to adopt the use of self as a therapeutic tool, listening skills, self awareness, handling feelings,

interpersonal and intrapersonal issues, counselling skills and behavioural skills. It also entails supervision of patients, working with anxious, depressed, aggressive, confused, dying, bereaved, institutionalised, overactive, hallucinating and deluded people either on an individual basis or in groups in a home or community setting. This requires considerable skill and organisation on the part of the psychiatric nurse."

2.24 A number of submissions referred to the changes in the provision of psychiatric nursing care in the years since the publication of the document *Planning for the Future*. The changes that had taken place and the role of psychiatric nurses in facilitating these changes was recognised in the *Green Paper on Mental Health* published in 1992. This stated; *"The changes have radically altered the working lives of many nurses and placed demands on them with which they were ill-equipped by their training to deal"*. Many psychiatric nurses suggested that it was now time to review the role of psychiatric nurses and the legislative framework in which they operate.

2.25 Community psychiatric nursing emerged as a feature of the Irish health services in the 1960s. During this period the development of new drugs for the treatment of certain conditions allowed for the discharge to the community of patients from mental health institutions. However, a number of such patients had to be readmitted to the institutions following the re-emergence of psychotic symptoms. The most significant reason for the return of such symptoms was identified as non-compliance with the new medication, together with poor preparation of the families to accept the recovered patient back home from the institution. In response to these and other needs the establishment of a new grade of Community Psychiatric Nurse was deemed necessary to enable the smooth transition of patients from institutions into the community.

2.26 The publication of *Planning for the Future* as stated earlier resulted in a reorientation of mental health services in this country with an even greater emphasis on community services. It was stated that increased numbers of psychiatric nurses were now working in the community and many community psychiatric nurses in submissions to the Commission requested the continuance and review of the grade and their role.

Relationship between Nurses and Medical Practitioners

2.27 The relationship between nurses and medical practitioners was also raised during the course of the consultative process undertaken by the Commission. While relationships generally were considered positive, a number of nurses suggested that some medical practitioners did not treat their nursing colleagues with the respect required to promote an effective working relationship. Cultural differences, in relation to attitudes to women, were also seen as giving rise to difficulties in the relationship between some doctors and nurses. The medical bodies, mentioned in paragraph 1.13, which met with the Commission, indicated their wish to maintain and promote an effective working relationship with the nursing profession and to offer support in the development of nursing. Unfortunately, the Irish Hospital Consultants Association and the Royal College of Psychiatrists in Ireland were unable to meet the Commission prior to the publication of the Interim Report.

CHAPTER 3

Preparation for the Profession

The Apprenticeship Model of Training

3.1 The traditional model of pre-registration training and education for nurses has been described as an "apprenticeship" model. This system, regardless of discipline, was based on classroom instruction and practical training, predominantly in a hospital setting. The arrangement of student nurse training consisted of a student working on a ward and attending lectures. It was mainly characterised by a hospital based training pattern where the student was an employee and part of the staffing complement of a hospital. The examination and assessment system consisted of continuous assessment of clinical skills through a proficiency assessment format and a final written examination conducted by An Bord Altranais.

3.2 Formerly a student seeking to become a nurse could enter one of four nursing pre-registration programmes — general, psychiatric, sick children's and mental handicap nursing. After successful completion of one programme and registration, a further eighteen month programme could be undertaken in order to register in another of these four disciplines of nursing. However, following the EU Directive 89/595/EEC, availability of such shorter courses became limited. A recent change to these education pathways was the requirement of registration as a general, psychiatric or mental handicap nurse in order to pursue an education programme in sick children's nursing. Following registration and experience in one of these four disciplines of nursing, a nurse can pursue an education programme to seek registration as a nurse tutor. Registration as a general nurse is required to pursue an education programme in midwifery and registration as a midwife is required to pursue an education programme in public health nursing.

3.3 An Bord Altranais under the Nurses Act 1985, is charged with the responsibility for the control of nurse education. The system operates and is controlled under the Nurses Rules 1988 (as amended), and criteria for the implementation of the syllabi of training. An Bord Altranais' criteria provide guidance to schools of nursing on the implementation of their programme of nurse education and training. The criteria established by An Bord Altranais must fulfil the European Union Directives on general nursing and midwifery. There are currently no EU Directives on sick children's, mental handicap and psychiatric nursing. Individual schools of nursing are monitored through an inspection system by An Bord Altranais, such an inspection being carried out at least once every five years in accordance with the Nurses Rules 1988.

New Diploma Programme

3.4 The apprenticeship model was evaluated by An Bord Altranais and a number of weaknesses were identified which militated against a beneficial experience for the student nurse. These included a lack of preparedness for certain duties, a lack of clinical teaching, an emphasis on work rather than learning and an involvement in non-nursing duties. In the light of this evaluation the traditional apprenticeship model of pre-registration nurse training and education has been replaced by a new diploma based programme in general, psychiatric and mental handicap nursing. The diploma based pre-registration education programme is offered by schools of nursing in association with colleges/universities. The objective of the transition to the new programme was to enhance nursing education and training. This was in line with key recommendations contained in the report *The Future of Nurse Education and Training in Ireland* published by An Bord Altranais in 1994.

Main Features of the New Diploma Programme

3.5 The main features of the registration/diploma programme have been described as:

- selection of applicants for places in schools of nursing offering the programme through the national Nursing Applications Centre (see paragraph below);

- students on the programme register with the associated university/college as well as on the candidate register of An Bord

30

Altranais, and have access to the facilities of the university/college;

- the associated university/college validates the curriculum and provides up to 500 lecture hours in the areas of biological and social sciences to the first year students;

- students are examined and assessed by the associated university/college throughout the programme in addition to undergoing the examination and assessment procedures prescribed in the Rules of An Bord Altranais;

- the third level fees are funded by the Department of Health and paid through the relevant health board/hospital/agency;

- students on the programme are supernumerary to service requirements and are not therefore paid a salary;

- the existing "traditional" student nurses' service is replaced by an appropriate grade/skill mix of registered nurses and other grades;

- students receive a maintenance grant of £2,500 per annum paid in monthly instalments;

- principal textbooks up to a value of £200 are supplied to students without charge by the participating schools of nursing at the commencement of the programme;

- students are also supplied with uniforms purchased for them by the health board/hospital/agency;

- students are provided with free meals on a seven day per week basis;

- students are responsible for arranging their own accommodation and an accommodation officer is available to assist and advise them after offers of places on the programme have been accepted.

3.6 The registration/diploma programme conforms to the syllabus and rules of An Bord Altranais and relevant EU Directives. The arrangements that have been put in place between the schools of nursing and the university/college participating in the programme involve the schools of nursing remaining as distinct entities within the health services. Generally, the Matron/Director of Nursing retains overall responsibility for the school of nursing which is managed by a Principal Nurse Tutor. The associated universities/colleges have each established a department/centre of nursing studies which is a distinct entity within the institute. This department/centre of nursing studies is managed by a nurse with appropriate academic qualifications and experience.

Course Programme

3.7 The programme is of 156 weeks duration (3 consecutive years) and meets the 4,600 hours of theoretical and clinical instruction required by the rules of An Bord Altranais and specified in the terms of EU Directive 89/595/EEC. The theory content of the programme (including study time) is of 58 weeks duration. A total of 86 weeks is allocated to clinical placements (nursing practice). Clinical placement co-ordinators have been appointed in each training hospital/agency to advise, encourage and facilitate students to achieve the maximum benefit from clinical placements. Nursing practice development co-ordinators have also been appointed to help ensure the optimum learning environment for student nurses on clinical placement, in addition to other nursing practice functions.

Nursing Schools Providing the Diploma Programme

3.8 The first nursing registration/diploma programme, following approval by An Bord Altranais, commenced on a pilot basis in University College Hospital, Galway, in association with University College Galway, in October, 1994. The programme of education commenced in University College Hospital Galway became known as the "Galway Model". The programme was extended to four schools of nursing in 1995. The programme was further extended to nine additional schools of nursing in 1996 and to thirteen additional schools of nursing in 1997. Twenty seven schools of nursing now offer a pre-registration nursing diploma programme based on the "Galway Model". The remaining schools of nursing, of which there are a small number in mental handicap and psychiatry, are expected to complete the transition to the diploma programme in 1998.

Evaluation of Programme

3.9 In April, 1996 a comprehensive independent external evaluation of the "Galway Model" registration/diploma programme commenced. This is being undertaken by Professor Helen Simons and a team from the School of Education and Nursing, University of Southampton, under the management of the Institute of Public Administration. The evaluation includes both the general nursing and psychiatric nursing programmes. This exercise is due to be completed in June, 1998. However, an interim report has recently been completed and has been made available by the Department of Health to the Commission for its consideration.

Nursing Applications Centre

3.10 In 1995 the Minister for Health established the Nursing Applications Centre on a pilot basis to provide a single application and selection system for applicants seeking places on the new pre-registration nursing diploma programme. The Nursing Applications Centre has managed three annual intakes to the programme.

3.11 The Department of Health informed the Commission that it has engaged Price Waterhouse Management Consultants to carry out an evaluation of the Nursing Applications Centre with the overall aim of ensuring that the most up-to-date application and selection procedures are employed, with maximum equity and effectiveness. Price Waterhouse acted as project managers for the application/selection process for the 1997 student intake as part of their evaluation of the current procedures. This arrangement was intended to facilitate the introduction, on an experimental basis, of certain modifications to the procedures employed in previous years with the objective of streamlining the application/selection process. Price Waterhouse will report to the Department of Health and make recommendations after the completion of the 1997 student intake. It has come to the attention of the Commission that there are many concerns in relation to the Nursing Applications Centre and the system it operates.

Issues raised during the Consultative Process

3.12 The introduction of the diploma programme was widely welcomed as offering new educational opportunities for the nursing profession. It was seen as beginning the process of placing the education of nurses on a par with that of other professions in the health services. The diploma programme was also seen as possibly leading to a more broadly educated, more analytical and self-confident profession whilst retaining the core value of caring for patients.

3.13 However, numerous concerns were expressed to the Commission in relation to the current model of the pre-registration diploma programme both by those attending the consultative fora organised by the Commission and in written submissions. As indicated earlier the first pre-registration nursing diploma programme commenced as a pilot scheme at University College Hospital Galway in association with University College Galway in 1994 and became known as the "Galway model". The "Galway model" pre-registration nursing diploma programme was extended to other schools of nursing as a condition of funding by the Department of Health. Much of the criticism is directed at the decision to instigate an extension of the "Galway model" prior to its full evaluation and in the absence of consultation with nurse tutors, other educationalists and the universities/colleges in relation to the curriculum, the nature of the academic award to be granted and the relationship of schools of nursing with universities/college departments and An Bord Altranais.

3.14 It was suggested to the Commission that due to the fact that all of the biological/social science subjects taught by the universities/colleges, together with a substantial amount of nursing theory and practice, must be given during the first year of the diploma programme, excessive demands were placed on students. It was argued that this overload of academic material has lead to difficulties throughout the second and third year of the programme. Diploma students are required to sit two exams, one for their Diploma and one for An Bord Altranais in order to be registered as nurses. It was submitted to the Commission that there was a need to:

- ensure that as a main objective, the new programme continued to produce nurses who were caring and patient centred;

- reduce the overall assessment burden on first year pre-registration diploma programme students;

- align the respective assessment regimes of An Bord Altranais and the relevant third level institutions;

- circumvent obstacles to the alignment of the academic calendars and appeal systems of An Bord Altranais and the relevant third level institutions; and

- facilitate the linking of theory to practice.

3.15 Two sets of criteria were identified as impinging on the basic education of nurses. These were:

- EU Directives for nurses responsible for general care; and

- An Bord Altranais rules for education and training.

3.16 It was suggested that the relevant EU Directives on the education of nurses responsible for general care have been interpreted in this country as meaning that those providing such education must satisfy the criteria of a minimum of a three year course and 4,600 hours of theoretical and clinical instruction, even though they are expressed as alternatives. Article 1(2)(b) of Directive 77/453/EEC reads:

> *"full-time training, of a specifically vocational nature, which must cover the subjects of the training programme set out in the Annex to this Directive and comprise a three year course or 4600 hours of theoretical and practical instruction."*

It was argued that the interpretation adopted in this country has resulted in those providing the three year diploma programme having to fit 4,600 hours of theoretical and clinical instruction into a three year programme in which the timetable consists of theoretical instruction weeks of thirty hours duration and clinical instruction weeks of even longer duration. Such a programme was considered excessively demanding on students and it was stated in submissions, at variance with best educational practice.

3.17 In addition, it was suggested that An Bord Altranais' rules on education and training impose excessive rigidity on the education programme and its assessment. It was further indicated that those responsible for planning nursing education programmes were excessively constrained by these rules and that educational principles and quality issues had to be set aside in the task of fulfilling them.

3.18 Concerns were also expressed that student nurses were not seen as real university/college students. They are not located on the university campus and this fact together with the amount of time they spend receiving instruction militates against their interaction with other students. It was suggested that part of the benefit of a university based education was the interaction with other students and the exchange of ideas with students studying a variety of subjects. The grant provided to nursing students was seen as insufficient, particularly when students were on clinical placements. Student nurses were required to attend theoretical or clinical instruction throughout the calendar year (except for 20 days holidays) and they therefore were unable to avail of opportunities for part-time or holiday employment open to other university students to maintain themselves during the academic year.

3.19 Some submissions suggested that responsibility for the funding of the pre-registration nursing programme should lie with the Department of Education through the Higher Education Authority.

3.20 Concern was expressed generally in relation to the selection criteria for student nurses. A suggestion was that if interview boards were retained that universities should be represented on such boards. Another suggestion was that Leaving Certificate performance should be recognised for entry purposes and that possibly the Central Applications Office be used. The requirement of a third language for entry into the nursing diploma programme was raised as an issue by career guidance teachers.

3.21 A particular concern expressed by psychiatric nurses was the small number of students opting for psychiatric nurse training. The view was also expressed that the number of places available was inadequate.

Nurse Tutors

3.22 The move from an apprenticeship model of education to a diploma programme, it was suggested, has impacted on the role of nurse tutors. Academic institutions expect nurse tutors to participate in curriculum development and validation, as well as setting and marking exams with external examiners. It was suggested that the increasing academic emphasis in nursing education meant that nurse tutors should be treated on a par with that of college lecturers. The issue of who should have overall responsibility for schools of nursing was also raised during the consultative process. It was argued in a number of submissions that schools of nursing should be the responsibility of nurse educators and that a nurse educator should have responsibility for the management and direction of a school of nursing. It was also submitted that highly qualified nurse tutors have been lost from nursing schools to positions in management and universities/colleges because of the absence of a strategic plan for nurse educators and nurse education.

Status of Existing Registered Nurses and Diploma Nurses

3.23 Nurses registered under the traditional apprenticeship model and diploma nurses have equal status under EU Directives and under conditions of employment in the Irish health services. Many registered nurses educated under the traditional apprenticeship model expressed concern at the impact of the diploma programme on the status of their nursing qualification. It was felt that preference would be given to diploma nurses in future promotional competitions. Registered nurses, through their post registration prior learning (not yet defined) will be eligible to apply for entry to a degree programme in nursing. Universities/colleges, in accordance with the normal procedures applying to such institutes, are developing a one year degree programme for students who successfully register with An Bord Altranais and gain the Diploma in Nursing from any of the participating universities/colleges. Registered nurses who do not have prior learning which can be accredited at diploma level by the third level institute can become eligible for entry to the degree programme in some universities/colleges by successfully completing a short access programme. It is a requirement of approval by the Department of Health of any funding arrangement with a university/college that it offers access programmes to existing registered nurses who do not meet the degree entry requirements. The first such access programme was commenced by Dublin City University in September, 1996. It is expected that any access course run by other third level institutes will be of similar duration and credit value to that agreed between the Department of Health and Dublin City University. However, it was suggested that varying requirements were emerging in different universities/colleges.

3.24 Whilst the provision of opportunities for non-diploma registered nurses to enter degree programmes was recognised by nurses, many suggested that given their age profile, family commitments, cost, distance from universities/colleges and the lack of study leave/staff replacement, these courses did not in fact offer a practical option. Many submissions requested that registered nurses without a diploma should be automatically granted one, recognising their experiential learning and the fact that they did not have an opportunity to pursue a pre-registration diploma programme under the traditional nursing education system.

State Enrolled Nurses

3.25 The Commission received a number of submissions from state enrolled nurses regarding conversion courses to become registered nurses. The state enrolled nurse is a United Kingdom qualification which is not recognised in Ireland. During the Depression in the 1930s, registered nurses were regarded as an expensive commodity and individual hospitals began to train assistant nurses to deliver at a lower cost some of the duties of registered nurses. The government in the United Kingdom reacted to this development by enacting the Nurses Act, 1943. This provided for a second level nurse, the state enrolled nurse, with a two year training programme, lower entry qualifications and whose duties were envisaged to be to assist the registered nurse in practical nursing care. The state enrolled nurse qualification came to be regarded as anomalous in the United Kingdom in the 1970s and 1980s and training courses for this grade were abolished. Subsequently, conversion courses to registered nurse status became more widely available. The United Kingdom Central Council for Nurses, Midwives and Health Visiting (UKCC) recognises the state enrolled nurse qualification alone as sufficient to access conversion courses. A number of state enrolled nurses who are employed in the Irish health services have asked An Bord Altranais to assess their qualification and provide appropriate conversion courses in Ireland to allow them the opportunity to convert to registered nurse status in this country.

Nurses Trained Abroad

3.26 Not all nurses undertake their pre-registration training in this country. Many of them train in the United Kingdom and return to make a significant contribution to the nursing profession in this country. Many of the nurses drew on their professional experience abroad, particularly that gained in the UK, when making their submissions.

CHAPTER 4

Professional Development

4.1 A common theme from workshops during the consultative fora and in written submissions was the wish of nurses to extend the parameters of their professional practice. Many nurses considered that they were constrained from performing tasks which they suggested were within their professional competence such as suturing, intravenous cannulation and the administration of non-controlled drugs, such as Calpol, without a prescription from a medical practitioner. In addition, it was suggested that there was a need for a clinical career pathway. It was considered that current nursing promotional structures force nurses away from the bedside and the patient and into roles in administration or teaching. It was also suggested that current nursing career pathways failed to recognise the reality of developments in the health services where increasing numbers of nurses concentrated their practice in particular areas and became highly skilled in those areas. It was submitted that there was increasing demand for "specialist" nurses. The wish of all nurses to expand the parameters of their professional practice and to have career opportunities in clinical practice, it was suggested, was also reflected in an increased demand for opportunities for continuing education and for further research to underpin nursing practice.

The Expanding Role of all Nurses

4.2 Nursing care is provided in a great variety of settings from highly technical acute hospital settings with multi-disciplinary support to community hospitals with limited support to individual practitioners visiting family homes. All nurses, however, expressed a wish to have opportunities to extend the parameters of their professional practice. Examples were given of nurses working in community hospitals with no medical support on site having to ring general practitioners to obtain prescriptions in order to administer a non-controlled drug which the patient or his/her relative could administer at home without prescription. Other examples were given of nurses working in acute hospitals wishing to have opportunities to perform activities such as intravenous cannulation. Similarly public health nurses wished to be able to make direct referrals to other professionals such as speech therapists without having to go through general practitioners or to prescribe specific dressings for wounds when assessment deemed it appropriate. The basis for this wish to extend the parameters of nursing practice was not to upgrade the "status" of nursing, it was suggested, but rather was underpinned by a strong wish to provide good quality and appropriate nursing care to patients and to alleviate suffering. It was submitted that the expanding role/activites which nurses wished to perform were those which they felt competent to undertake.

4.3 It became clear during the consultative fora organised by the Commission that the parameters of nursing practice vary throughout the country. In large acute Dublin hospitals many nurses appeared to be given opportunities to extend their practice in areas such as suturing whilst in other hospitals it seemed that nursing practice was severely constrained by the lack of enabling local policies and protocols. There appeared to be a view that both the current health care and professional systems did not provide the opportunities, scope or support for all nurses to extend their practice.

4.4 The role of An Bord Altranais in relation to the development of nursing practice received much criticism. It was felt that An Bord Altranais did not offer sufficient support to nurses to develop their practice and in some cases was seen as further constraining practice. It appeared guidance on such issues was sought from employing authorities and An Bord Altranais out of concern that nurses extending their practice might encounter litigation or have to appear before the Fitness to Practise Committee of An Bord Altranais. The issues relating to the regulation of the nursing profession will be considered in Chapter Five of this report.

A Clinical Career Pathway

4.5 The current career pathway for nurses offers opportunities for them to advance their career either as nurse managers or as nurse educators.

It was argued that there were no opportunities for nurses who wished to advance their career in clinical practice and remain at the bedside of the patient. An Bord Altranais' publication in 1997 entitled *Continuing Professional Education for Nurses in Ireland: A Framework* offered a possible career pathway for nurses composed of pathways in education, clinical practice, management or research. This career structure was broadly welcomed by nurses both at consultative fora and in written submissions.

4.6 It seemed from submissions that there were large numbers of nurses who considered themselves to be "specialists" in particular areas of nursing practice. Many of these nursing "specialities" seemed to develop in response to demands for more specialised nurses from medical practitioners to support more effectively patients with medical conditions such as diabetes, cystic fibrosis and renal disease. However, a number of other areas which might be regarded as nursing "specialities" appeared to develop in response to the demands of changes in nursing practice, such as in pain management, continence management and behavioural psychotherapy. Nurses working in specialised areas appeared to have more autonomy and in many instances felt empowered and enabled to initiate changes in medication or treatment for patients within their area of practice. It is not intended here to identify any specialities in nursing, just to state that a wide variety appear to have developed on an almost ad-hoc basis over the years. These "specialist" nurses appeared to be graded at a variety of levels from staff nurse to ward sister. There seemed from the submissions received by the Commission to be little coherence in the selection of nurses for "specialist" areas and little coherence in the recognition of nurses as "specialists" either by their peers, nursing management, medical professionals or general management. No framework seemed to exist for the creation or recognition of nursing specialities.

4.7 It was suggested that one of the advantages of "specialist" nurses supporting a medical consultant was that they develop great expertise and provide continuity of care to the patient. This was because they were assigned to one unit and one group of patients in one hospital unlike non-consultant hospital doctors who rotate and unlike consultants who may work in a number of hospitals and may have duties in other medical areas as well. "Specialist" nurses provide accessibility and continuity of care which medical practitioners may not be in a position to provide and so become the patients first point of contact in times of crisis.

4.8 It should be noted that caution was expressed during the consultative process in relation to the term "Advanced Practitioner". It was suggested that this may result in the development of a certain elitism amongst a category of nurses and more importantly may by degrees result in other nurses providing general nursing care to become seen as "basic" nurses. It was argued that the perception of those nurses providing general nursing care, which should remain at the core of nursing, being viewed as "basic" nurses was something that must be avoided if the profession was to retain its unity and coherence. Nursing appeared to have been traditionally regarded as a very hierarchical profession and the view was offered during the consultative process that developments in advanced practice should not be seen as adding hierarchical layers but rather as a resource and opportunity for all nurses and a benefit to patients.

4.9 There is a range of issues in relation to the development of a career pathway for nurses in clinical practice. These include:

- the relationship between specialist/advanced nursing practitioners and nursing management;

- the relationship between specialist/advanced nursing practitioners and medical practitioners, particularly non-consultant hospital doctors; and

- the level or grade of specialist/advanced nursing practitioner grades;

- the education and experience required from "specialist" status.

Continuing Professional Education

4.10 Continuing professional education was the focus of much discussion at the consultative fora and was raised in numerous written submissions to the Commission. It was felt that the nursing profession needed to be able to respond in an effective and proactive manner to the ever increasing pace of change and development in the health services. The means of ensuring the on-going capacity of the nursing profession to develop and respond to changing health care needs, it was suggested, was through a comprehensive and coherent system of continuing professional education. Many nurses welcomed the document *Continuing Professional Education: A Framework* published by An Bord Altranais in 1997. The definition of continuing professional education adopted by An Bord Altranais in the document was:

> *"Continuing education is a life-long professional development process which takes place after the completion of the pre-registration nurse education programme. It consists of planned learning experiences which are designed to augment the knowledge, skills and attitudes of registered nurses for the enhancement of nursing practice, patient/client care, education, administration and research."*

4.11 A number of health boards informed the Commission of developments in continuing nurse education in recent years. The most recent of these was the appointment of nurse education co-ordinators in several health boards and it was reported that large numbers of nurses were availing of continuing education opportunities. An Bord Altranais in their submission to the Commission stated that they would establish:

- a National Advisory Committee on Continuing Professional Education representative of the various interests involved in continuing professional education in Ireland;

- a specialist Continuing Education Unit in An Bord Altranais with responsibility inter alia for carrying out research on, and evaluation of, continuing education programmes;

- an accreditation framework to ensure that a system of mutual recognition and credit accumulation and transfer is agreed between the higher education institutions; and

- a recording system of post-registration courses.

4.12 Continuing professional education may take a number of forms; in-service training, career development and personal/professional development. In-service training allows nurses to become aware of developments in nursing practice for example in challenging behaviour and infection control. Courses which provide for career development might be in an area such as theatre nursing which would allow a nurse to focus her career pathway on a particular aspect of clinical nursing. A number of nurses take courses outside the nursing area, such as law courses, for reasons of personal/professional development. Such courses provide opportunities for nurses to extend their area of knowledge beyond nursing and may provide further opportunities in nursing or elsewhere. It was suggested that many nurses were currently taking courses in a great variety of areas without any clear focus. Similarly, there was no recognition of their efforts in maintaining or upgrading their professional competence. Sometimes there appeared to be little differentiation between in-service training and career development, particularly in some "specialist" areas where nurses received additional training on-site and "on the job". A need was identified for more career guidance.

4.13 There was a view that since there was a lack of clear focus in terms of career development, there appeared to be a culture developing of what might be described as "qualification inflation" in nursing, whereby nurses were acquiring additional qualifications merely to be able to compete for various posts. This appeared to be exacerbating the frustration felt by many nurses in relation to equity concerning the availability of, and funding for courses.

4.14 It was stated that great efforts were made by nurses in acquiring additional skills and the opportunities to use such skills might not be readily available, yet the absence of additional qualifications was seen as a disadvantage in competing for nursing posts. An example was given of nurses acquiring an additional midwifery qualification because of the perception that such a qualification was desirable when applying for a general nurse post in some small hospitals. A view was expressed that an effort needed to be made to try and match continuing education and development by nurses with assessed need.

4.15 Whilst many nurses were availing of opportunities to upgrade their skills, other nurses appeared either not to have had opportunities to avail of continuing education or chose not to do so. It was claimed that many nurses had to upgrade their skills on their own time and because of work, family and other commitments some nurses were not able to devote their spare time to further professional education. In addition, nurses outside of Dublin expressed concern in relation to the availability and geographic accessibility of further education courses. There was a view that the "substantial" clinically based courses which would provide greater career opportunities were only available in Dublin. There was a call for improved access to further education and the greater use of more innovative education approaches such as the use of distance learning techniques. The provision of further nursing education programmes in locations more accessible to nurses was suggested.

4.16 Access to further professional education also raised the issue of study leave and the payment of course fees. The view was expressed that study leave and the payment of course fees was provided on an ad-hoc basis with little consistency or equity both between organisations and within organisations. A nurse might also not be allowed to avail of an opportunity for further professional education because of staff replacement difficulties. The provision of staff cover for nurses on study leave seemed to be particularly difficult in the smaller hospitals and in the community. The difficulty in obtaining study leave from employers seemed to underpin a number of calls for mandatory study leave. It was argued that an entitlement to study leave would ensure that employers allowed all nurses to avail of opportunities to upgrade their professional skills and ensure greater equity in the granting of study leave. There was also a view that nurses should be required to regularly update their skills as a pre-requisite to continuing registration with An Bord Altranais.

4.17 Nurses complained that there was little recognition for additional qualifications either by employers or An Bord Altranais. Many nurses were of the view that an additional allowance should be paid to nurses if they acquired additional post-registration qualifications. Some suggested this should be paid irrespective of the relevance of the additional qualification to the nurses area of practice. There was also complaint that An Bord Altranais did not record on the register qualifications outside the currently registerable nursing disciplines, namely; General, Psychiatric, Mental Handicap, Sick Children's, Public Health, Midwifery and Tutor. It was argued that this failure to register additional qualifications impinged on manpower planning. It was very difficult, for example, to determine the number of nurses in Ireland who might have a post-registration anaesthetic qualification.

Management Development

4.18 Some nurses during the course of the consultative process were of the view that little management training and development was provided for nurses. It was suggested that nurses in senior nursing management positions had received inadequate management training and that there was an over reliance on "on the job" development. It was recognised, however, that many senior nurse managers had acquired considerable management skills in the process. It was felt that there were few continuing education opportunities to engender or develop management skills amongst nurses. This issue will be dealt with in more detail in Chapter Six.

Information Technology and Services

4.19   The use of information technology has become increasingly prevalent in the health services as in all other areas of Irish society. Nurses identified a need to make greater use of information technology and for increased training in its use. It was felt that with improved training nurses would be able to make better use of existing information technology and possibly identify additional areas to which its use could be productively extended and thus improve patient care.

4.20   The demand for continuing education was also identified as leading to an increased demand for improved library facilities for nurses. It was felt that existing library facilities did not sufficiently support nurses in their continuing professional education or their desire simply to keep up to date with nursing developments. The view was expressed that greater use of nursing databases would assist nurses in their practice, provided such databases were readily accessible.

Research

4.21   Many nurses, in discussions at the consultative fora and in written submissions to the Commission, identified the need for developments in nursing research. It was suggested that if the nursing profession was to develop there was an increasing need for nursing practice to be underpinned by research. Nursing needed to examine its processes and explore the effectiveness and efficiency of alternative approaches. The transition from pre-registration nursing education to a diploma programme was seen as offering opportunities for a greater emphasis on nursing research. The greater academic emphasis in nursing education would create an environment which would encourage greater questioning amongst nurses and the self-confidence to critically examine and explore new ways of nursing. The association with universities/colleges would also encourage the development of research because of the already highly developed "research culture" amongst other health science departments in universities/colleges.

4.22 The need to develop research as an integral part of the nursing service was identified in the report of the *Working Party on General Nursing* published by the Department of Health in 1980. However, it seems little development of nursing research has taken place in the intervening years. It was suggested that funding was required for both nursing research projects and the development of nurse researchers.

4.23 It was also argued that there was a need to provide appropriate leadership in nursing research to ensure good quality research which in turn would lead to good quality decisions on nursing issues. It was suggested that there was a need to equip more nurses with the necessary research skills up to Ph.D level and to develop the practice of nursing research. Without properly focused and supported leadership, it was argued, bad practices could develop in nursing research.

4.24 There was a call for structures to be put in place which would encourage, support and develop nursing research. There was also a call to ensure more effective mechanisms were in place to disseminate the findings of nursing research. There was a view that nursing research was less successful in attracting funding than medical research.

CHAPTER 5

Regulation of the Nursing Profession

5.1 The nursing profession is primarily regulated pursuant to the Nurses Act 1985 (the 1985 Act). This Act repealed the Nurses Acts of 1950 and 1961 and sections of the Midwives Act 1944. It provided for the establishment a new Board to provide for the regulation, control and education of nurses and other matters related to the practice of nursing. The new Board established under the 1985 Act is known as An Bord Altranais. Under the 1985 Act a nurse means; *"a woman or man whose name is entered in the register and includes a midwife and "nursing" includes "midwifery"."* Prior to the Nurses Act 1950 there had been an independent board for the regulation of midwives.

5.2 The European Union has issued a number of directives affecting general nursing and midwifery, the general purpose of which is to enable general nurses and midwives to practise their profession in any member state. Directives 77/452/EEC and 77/453/EEC deal with general nursing whilst Directive 80/155/EEC deals with midwifery. The directives are concerned with mutual recognition of formal qualifications of nurses responsible for care and aim to ensure a comparatively high standard of training of nursing personnel throughout the Union. In 1989 a Directive from the Council of European Communities (89/595/EEC) amended Directives 77/452/EEC and 77/453/EEC.

An Bord Altranais

5.3 The main functions of An Bord Altranais under the 1985 Act relate to:

- the maintenance of a register of nurses;

- the control of education and training of student nurses and the post-registration training of nurses;

- the operation of the fitness to practise procedures; and

- the ensuring of compliance with European Union Directives on nursing and midwifery.

An Bord Altranais has as its general concern under the 1985 Act the promotion of *"high standards of professional education and training and professional conduct among nurses"*. The present board of An Bord Altranais consists of twenty-nine members, seventeen of whom are nurses elected by the nursing profession and the remainder are appointed by the Minister for Health and are drawn from the medical profession, the management of the health services, education interests and the general public. The composition of the board may be varied by regulations made by the Minister for Health after consultation with the board. The 1985 Act also provides for the appointment of a chief executive officer and other staff of An Bord Altranais.

Fitness to Practise

5.4 An Bord Altranais is required under the 1985 Act to establish a Fitness to Practise Committee, all of the members of which must be members of the board, a majority of whom must be elected members and one third of whom must be non-elected members. The 1985 Act confers on An Bord Altranais powers to inquire into complaints against members of the nursing profession regarding their fitness to practice either for professional misconduct or because of physical or mental disability. An Bord Altranais has power to remove or suspend the name of a nurse for a period or attach conditions to the retention of the name of a nurse on the register. There must then be an application to the High Court which may confirm, cancel or vary the decision of An Bord Altranais. In addition, the Board may advise, admonish or censure nurses in relation to professional conduct.

5.5 The nursing profession also operates within the parameters of legislation other than the 1985 Act. In the area of professional practice these include the Misuse of Drugs Acts 1977 and 1984, the Health (Nursing Homes) Act 1990, the Child Care Act 1991 and the Data Protection Act

1988. In addition, nurses are becoming increasingly aware of their civil liability in the area of the law of negligence.

5.6 The Misuse of Drugs Acts set out detailed provisions on the storage, dispensing and administration of controlled drugs. Controlled drugs comprise scheduled and dangerous drugs. It is a criminal offence to be in breach of the Misuse of Drugs Acts. An Bord Altranais also issued a document — *Guidance to Nurses and Midwives on the Administration of Medical Preparations* — to assist nurses in relation to the administration of medical preparations, the fourth edition of which was published in 1997.

5.7 The Health (Nursing Homes) Act 1990 updated the law on nursing homes with the aim of ensuring high standards of care. Under this Act a new framework was put in place for the exercising of responsibilities by nurses working in nursing homes and in the community. The Child Care Act 1991 updated the law on the protection of children and places certain statutory obligations on those health care personnel working, or in contact, with children. This Act has particular importance for public health nurses working with families in the community. Nurses are affected by the Data Protection Act 1988 when dealing with issues on the confidentiality of computerised patient records and by the Freedom of Information Act 1997 when dealing with patient records.

Issues Arising from the Consultative Process

5.8 As indicated above, nursing practice is regulated by a combination of a statutory professional regulatory body and other legislation. The general framework is similar to that for the medical profession which has a statutory regulatory body and is also governed by a range of other legislation.

5.9 It appeared from discussions at the consultative fora and from written submissions to the Commission that many nurses were dissatisfied with the nature and level of professional support offered by An Bord Altranais. It appeared that many nurses were of the view that An Bord Altranais did not take a sufficiently pro-active view in the development of nursing practice. It was also suggested that An Bord Altranais appeared to constrain practice in some areas and offered little guidance in other areas. Nurses were concerned about extending the parameters of professional nursing practice in the absence of clear guidance from their regulatory body. There were concerns that if professional issues were unclear now or in the future, nurses seeking to extend their practice could face investigation before the Fitness to Practise Committee. It was suggested during the consultative process that An Bord Altranais should empower nurses to a much greater extent to make professional decisions rather than have prescriptive guidelines in certain areas. The United Kingdom Central Council for Nursing, Midwifery and Health Visiting document — *The Scope of Professional Practice (1992)* — was given as an example of the empowerment of nurses on professional issues. This states that the principles which should govern adjustments to the scope of professional practice are that the registered nurse, midwife or health visitor:

"9.1 must be satisfied that each aspect of practice is directed to meeting the needs and serving the interests of the patient or client;

9.2 must endeavour always to achieve, maintain and develop knowledge, skill and competence to respond to needs and interests;

9.3 must honestly acknowledge any limits of personal knowledge and skill and take steps to remedy any relevant deficits in order effectively and appropriately to meet the needs of patients and clients;

9.4 must ensure that any enlargement or adjustment of the scope of personal professional practice must be achieved without compromising or fragmenting existing aspects of professional practice and care and that the requirements of the Council's Code of Professional Conduct are satisfied throughout the whole area of practice;

9.5 must recognise and honour the direct or indirect personal accountability borne for all aspects of professional practice; and

9.6 must, in serving the interests of patients and clients and the wider interests of society, avoid any inappropriate delegation to others which compromises those interests.

. . . . The practice of nursing has traditionally been based on the premise that pre-registration education equips the nurse to perform at a certain level and to encompass a particular range of activities. It is also based on the premise that any widening of that range and enhancements of the nurses's practice requires 'official' extension of that role by certification.

The Council considers that the terms 'extended' or 'extending' roles which have been associated with this system are no longer suitable since they limit, rather than extend, the parameters of practice. As a result, many practitioners have been prevented from fulfilling their potential for the benefit of patients. . . . . . "

5.10 An Bord Altranais in the — *Code of Professional Conduct for each Nurse and Midwife* — published in 1988 states that the nurse *"must acknowledge any limitations of competence and refuse in such cases to accept delegated functions without first having received instruction in regard to those functions and having been assessed as competent."*

5.11 The current framework appeared to be viewed as inadequate to allow nursing practice to respond to changes in the provision of health services and as not providing sufficient support to allow nurses confidently develop their professional practice.

5.12 Concerns were also expressed by nurses that An Bord Altranais did not appear to be involved in a pro-active manner in promoting the independent professional identity of nurses. It was suggested that nurses wished their regulatory body to more actively promote the distinct identity of nursing and to promote a greater sense of the "profession of nursing" amongst nurses.

5.13 In their submission to the Commission, An Bord Altranais recognised the wish of nurses to extend the parameters of their professional practice and their wish for a distinct role with greater autonomy, responsibility and accountability.

5.14 Nurses also expressed concern in relation to the perceived lack of independence of An Bord Altranais. There were some complaints in relation to the presence of representatives of the Department of Health, health services management and medical practitioners on the regulatory body for nurses. It was noted that there were no similar representatives on the regulatory body for medical practitioners.

5.15 The Commission received a number of submissions from pharmacists in relation to the *Medical Products (Prescription and Control of Supply) Regulations 1996*. It was stated that these regulations provide, for the first time in law, a specific entitlement for nurses to supply medicinal products in the course of a service provided by a hospital or supply medicinal products in a quantity sufficient for a period of treatment not exceeding three days, in the course of a service provided by a hospital delivering community mental health services to patients. It was suggested in submissions from pharmacists that nurses were not sufficiently competent to carry out the functions allowed to them under the regulations.

CHAPTER 6

The Role of Nurses in the Management of Services

6.1 In discussion at the consultative fora and in written submissions a variety of factors were identified as impacting on the Irish health services. These included a growing consumer movement and rising patient expectations, an increasing elderly population, advances in medical technology fuelling increased demand and cost and the need to account for the effective use of available resources. *Shaping a Healthier Future,* published by the Department of Health in 1994, was seen as encapsulating the changes underway in the health services. The Irish health services were perceived by nurses as operating in an environment of rapid change which required the effective integration of multi-discipline and multi-functional teams. Managers in the health services were seen as needing to be able to manage in a complex, changing environment and to manage the pace of change in this environment. Many nurses identified a need for strong nursing leadership as the health services develop and respond to changes. There was also a view that nursing management could not be considered in isolation from the broader health services.

The Role of Nurses in Planning, Policy and Strategy

6.2 A common theme during the consultative fora and in written submissions was the perception that nurses were not sufficiently involved in planning or in policy and strategy development. Nurses wished to have opportunities to contribute to the development of strategy and policy and to be involved in the corporate decision making process. The view was expressed that the current structures did not facilitate such opportunities. The appointment of a Chief Nursing Officer at the Department of Health was widely welcomed as commencing the process of more effectively involving nurses at policy making management levels in the health services. The view was expressed that a senior nurse should form part of the administrative structure at health board level. The perception of exclusion from strategic and policy development appeared to be shared by both nursing management and staff nurses. It was argued that the greater involvement of nurses in planning, policy and strategy development would give nurses a greater sense of identification with the "corporate goals" of health service providers and give a greater sense of commitment to the attainment of those goals. There was a view that policy makers in the health services needed to adopt a more consultative style and to create opportunities for nurses at management and staff nurse level to have an input into policy development.

6.3   The presence of two elected nursing representatives on each of the health boards was also discussed during the consultative process. Some nurses argued for increased nursing representation at health board level, others appeared unaware that there was such representation on health boards. A view was expressed by one senior nurse manager that his views on major nursing issues before the health board had never been sought by the nursing representative who appeared to concentrate exclusively on occupational health and other industrial relations issues. On the other hand, another senior nurse manager in another health board stated that she was regularly consulted on major policy issues before health board meetings.

Corporate Communication

6.4   In addition to the perception of insufficient involvement by nurses in the health service corporate decision making process, there was also a view that communication from general management to nurses and from nurses to general management needed improvement. There was a view that general management did not sufficiently appreciate the contribution and concerns of nurses and did not take sufficient account of the nursing perspective in reaching decisions. Similarly, there was a view that nurses were not sufficiently informed of the rationale for decisions which impacted on the delivery of nursing care to patients. It was suggested that there was a need for improved information flows through the health service management system to ensure that nurses were more involved and informed in the decision making process.

The Management of Nursing

6.5 The role of nursing management and the relationship between nurse managers, general managers, nurses and other professionals were raised during the consultative process. Nursing managers stated that they were constantly faced with the need to stay within budget. However, they argued that they had no involvement in setting the nursing budget and were often told that they had exceeded their budget without being informed of the budgetary figure at the outset or where they exceeded their budget. There appeared to be a lack of partnership and consultation between general management and nursing management and between nursing management and nurses in the setting and attaining of corporate goals. There was a view that nursing management lacked autonomy and could not take decisions in their area of responsibility in the absence of approval from general management. There appeared to be a sense of "helplessness" amongst some nurse managers because of the perception of their inability to influence the corporate decision making process. There was a view that nurse managers were asked simply to "manage down" and to implement the decisions of others without having any input or involvement in the decisions.

6.6 It was argued during the consultative process that senior nursing management, in general, focused on the individual management of nurses rather than the management of nursing. It was suggested that senior nursing management focused on such issues as the rostering of nurses, sick leave and annual leave rather than the development of nursing practice and policies for the more effective delivery of nursing care to patients. It was submitted to the Commission that some nursing managers were preoccupied with hierarchies and the detailed control of nurses rather than the management of the function of nursing. It was suggested that some nurse managers operated on the basis of command and control rather than consultation and the delegation of responsibility. There was a view that attitudes to and the attitude of some senior nurse managers were inherited from an era when there was a much greater emphasis on a hierarchical and insular structure of management. There was a view that this "system" produced a certain type of manager and that there was an absence of management training and development to prepare nurses for senior positions of authority.

Management Development

6.7 The Commission received a copy of the document — *A management development strategy for the health and personal social services in Ireland* — published by the Department of Health in December, 1996. Many of the issues, identified in that document as areas requiring development in relation to the overall management capability of the health services, were similarly suggested to the Commission as areas requiring examination in the role of nurses in the management of the health services. These included the development of those nurses with management potential, not only for nursing management but as a resource available to the health services in general, the need for improved succession planning for senior nurse management positions and concerns in relation to the system operated by the Local Appointments Commission (LAC) in the selection of nurses for senior nursing management positions. There was a view that the exclusion of the senior nurse manager in a hospital from the LAC interview process for his or her deputy or assistant matron did not facilitate the development of a management team and created difficulties in succession planning. It was further argued that the absence from the interview board of the senior nurse to whom the person would be reporting was exacerbated by the presence of inappropriate members on the interview board. The same criticisms were levelled at interviews set up by the health boards.

6.8 The Commission is aware of initiatives taken by the recently established Office for Health Management to help develop nursing managers. These include a Master Class for senior nurse management on "Effective Nurse Leadership: Making a Difference" and a leadership development programme for nurses under 35 years of age.

6.9 There was a view that the recruitment, selection and training of nurse managers needed to be examined in order to ensure that the nursing profession had an effective cohort of leaders capable of responding to the changing health service environment. It was suggested that the absence of clinical and other career pathways in nursing was resulting in many excellent clinical nurses pursuing managerial careers when perhaps their real talent lay in clinical practice. It was argued that those with managerial skills needed to be identified and developed to pursue a career in management and that formal mechanisms should be in place to allow for such development. Further, it was argued that nurses because of their educational background, experience and inter-personal skills offered a valuable "personnel pool" for the recruitment of general managers. It was suggested that nurses needed to be more aware of career opportunities outside of nursing in the management of the health services and that greater efforts should be made to inform nurses of such opportunities.

6.10 A submission identified a research study (O'Connor,1996) on perceived barriers to the promotion of women in two Irish health boards which found that nurses and paramedics perceived there to be a chasm between the largely female world of caring and the largely male world of administration. It also suggested that senior nurses and paramedics occupied positions of "high expertise" and "low authority" in the health boards insofar as they had very limited financial control and were very far removed from the real centres of power and decision making. This, it was alleged, was due to the largely female nature of these professions.

The Nursing Management Structure

6.11 Submissions in relation to the nursing management structure related to the roles and responsibilities of nursing management at various levels of the health service organisation. As stated earlier there was a view that there needed to be greater delegation of authority and responsibility through the layers of nursing management. The role and responsibility of a number of "deputy" management posts was discussed, these included posts such as deputy director of nursing and senior public health nurse. Given the perceived absence of delegation and the seeming involvement of senior nurse management in detail, rather than the management of the nursing function, there were calls for greater devolution of responsibility to first-line nursing managers. There was also debate in relation to the role and function of these "intermediate" management positions, as well as the overall structures most suitable for the management of the nursing function in the hospital and community.

6.12 The question of incentives for nurses to pursue a management career was raised in discussion at the consultative fora and in written submissions. The pay differentials across all nursing management positions were discussed during the consultative process as being insufficient to encourage talented individuals to seek nursing management posts. It was particularly argued that the current differentials between staff nurse posts and promotional posts were a disincentive to promotion. It was stated that because of the loss of premium payments for unsocial hours on promotion that those in first-line management positions were paid less than those in staff nurses positions at the upper end of the incremental pay scale. It was stated that the level of differential between staff nurse and promotional posts made it extremely difficult to attract nurses to seek promotion.

Ward Sisters

6.13 There was particular discussion in relation to the role and function of ward sisters. Some argued that the title "Ward Sister" was an anachronism and should be changed to "Ward Nurse Manager". There was also a view that there should be greater devolution of responsibility to ward sisters, that they should be given greater control over their own budget, a greater say in the determination of the budget and greater autonomy in the management of a ward. In order to develop the management function of the ward sister it was argued that such posts should be supernumerary, that is, not be required to carry out clinical functions as part of the staff complement on a ward. There was a view that ward sisters needed more management training if greater responsibility were to be devolved to them, particularly in the area of budget setting and management.

Management of Nursing in the Community

6.14 As outlined in chapter two there appeared to be increasing numbers of nurses working in the community in response to the greater emphasis throughout the health service on the improved provision of community care services. Community psychiatric nurses and public health nurses, as currently organised, have been working in the community since the 1960s. However, in recent years a number of "specialist nurses" have begun to work in the community, such as palliative care nurses. In addition, increasing numbers of general, psychiatric and mental handicap nurses have begun to work in the community. Practice nurses have begun to work in support of general practitioners.

6.15 A number of submissions raised the need to examine structures to ensure the effective provision of a community nursing service and the need to ensure an effective integrated working relationship between nurses of various disciplines working in the community.

CHAPTER 7

The Employment Conditions of Nurses

7.1 A series of issues were raised in the consultative fora and the written submissions received by the Commission, suggesting varying approaches to the employment of nurses between health boards and between hospitals/community care areas within a health board. This, the final chapter, sets out these issues as they were relayed to the Commission.

Temporary Nurses

7.2 The most prevalent issue relating to the employment of nurses was that of nurses employed in a temporary capacity. The Commission heard from many nurses who had worked full-time hours for many years without being appointed to a permanent post. Nurses described situations of repeatedly presenting for interview only to be placed so far down the list that it was impossible to be appointed during the life-time of the panel and some were not placed at all. Some nurses suggested that not being placed on a panel for permanent employment after working in a temporary capacity for a number of years adversely affected their morale. Yet, it was suggested, such nurses continued to be called in for duty at the convenience of the hospital despite being unsuccessful at interview. Many temporary nurses reported feeling undervalued, demoralised and very angry at such treatment.

7.3 It was submitted that long-term temporary nurses were denied many opportunities available to their permanent colleagues. The absence of such opportunities included lack of access to continuing education, lack of promotional prospects and the lack of pension. Some nurses complained that if they were not always available at very short notice to take up short-term employment, they were at risk of not being offered any further employment.

7.4 It was reported by many nurses that when eventually they were appointed to permanent posts further problems often arose. One issue was the backpayment of superannuation contributions for the years worked which, it was suggested, depending on the longevity of the temporary status, could amount to substantial payments over a relatively short period in order to gain full superannuation entitlements.

7.5 The issue of service increments arose during the consultative fora and also featured in the written submissions from temporary nurses. Temporary nurses believed that they were entitled to receive increments beyond the seventh point of the scale and proceed to the maximum of the pay scale.

7.6 During the consultative process examples were given of temporary nurses who, having spent years in a particular department (often it was suggested the only nurse with expertise in that area) were, on permanent appointment, re-deployed to another area of which they had little knowledge or experience and therefore minimal expertise. It was the opinion of these nurses that such redeployment did not make optimal use of their acquired skills.

7.7 It was noted by the Commission that the issue of temporary nurses did not appear to be as widespread a problem in the discussions at the consultative fora in the Dublin area compared with discussions/submissions from the rest of the country. One of the reasons for this, it was suggested, was the employment policies of large voluntary hospitals. This will be considered in greater detail and reported on in the final report.

Bullying

7.8 Many nurses in discussions at the consultative fora and in written submissions complained of bullying in the workplace. A definition of bullying provided to the Commission by the MSF union was that it involved *"persistent, offensive, abusive, intimidating, malicious or insulting behaviour, abuse of power or unfair penal sanctions, which makes the recipient feel upset, threatened, humiliated or vulnerable, which undermines their self-confidence and which may cause them to suffer* *stress."* It appeared that bullying may be taking place at a variety of levels in nursing. Complaints were made of students being bullied by nurses, nurses being bullied by other nurses and professionals, nurses being bullied by nurse management and nurse management being bullied by general management.

Staffing

7.9 It was suggested that nurse staffing levels in many places and in all disciplines throughout the country were inadequate and lacked uniformity. Although the issues of dependency ratios and the relationship of nurses and non-nursing personnel had been examined by some groups in recent years, there were no national criteria for determining staffing levels. Considerable dissatisfaction was expressed regarding the methods by which staffing levels were set. Nurses called for a uniform, transparent, equitable and objective method of determining staffing levels.

7.10 Among the many groups of nurses who reported inadequate staffing levels were public health nurses (PHNs) and nurses involved in care of the elderly. It was the belief of those working in care of the elderly, based in small district hospitals in particular, that staffing levels should reflect current patient needs and not continue to be based on historical needs (for example, welfare homes traditionally catered for the needs of well ambulant elderly). It was stated that patients being admitted for rehabilitation/respite care were nowadays much more dependent and required greater nursing intervention and care. It was suggested that changes in demography, technology, social factors and epidemiology in recent years required a review of staffing levels particularly in the area of public health nursing. PHNs reported a client base far in excess of what was considered appropriate. It was reported that an ever increasing workload without a corresponding increase in staffing levels was impacting on patient care and was placing undue stress on nurses.

7.11 It was stated that many specialised services had evolved over the years such as hospice care, stoma care and very often these services were provided by nurses working on their own. It was the opinion of some of these nurses that not only did they have a heavy caseload but they found it extremely difficult to avail of continuing education due to lack of locum cover.

Long Service Incentives

7.12 An issue which arose in discussions at the consultative fora and in written submissions was the question of incentives for those nurses with many years service in a particular grade. It was argued that some recognition should be given to those who had undertaken quality work for many years but who were not seeking promotion. Additional long service increments and/or increased holiday entitlements were suggested as possible incentives.

Flexible Working Arrangements

7.13 It was suggested that there was a need for greater flexibility in the hours worked by nurses at different levels. As a predominantly female profession it was believed that increased access to and availability of job sharing or permanent part-time work ought to be encouraged to allow nurses to combine satisfactorily their professional and family roles. Such flexibility in working arrangements was considered important in order to retain many highly qualified and competent nurses in the work force and it was suggested such arrangements should also extend to temporary nurses. The issue of the flexible employment of nurses approaching retirement in less physically demanding duties was also raised during the consultative process.

7.14 Some nurses also raised the issue of obstacles to transferring either between hospitals in a health board or between health boards where a suitable vacancy existed. They believed that the current system of having to repeat the entire selection process was unfair. In addition, some complained that having reached a certain increment level whilst employed in one health board they had to revert to the bottom of the incremental scale on taking up temporary employment with another health board. It was also stated that nurses were not able to transfer directly to a permanent post but had to take up temporary employment when moving between health boards or some hospitals within the same health board.

Personal Security

7.15 Many concerns were expressed at what was perceived as the lack of security afforded to nurses in particular situations, for example in the community and in isolated hospital settings. Nurses reported being subjected to both verbal and even physical abuse from clients or their relatives, particularly in accident and emergency departments. Public health nurses reported being exposed to threatening situations either in very isolated areas or in inner city areas with major socio-economic problems. It was stated that such nurses were very vulnerable as they were not equipped with mobile phones or personal alarms to enable them to call for help. It was submitted that nurses working in isolated settings felt particularly vulnerable at night. Some submissions from psychiatric nurses highlighted the increased exposure of nurses to violent behaviour. The relative isolation of some psychiatric units meant that sometimes there was no immediate back-up in crisis situations.

7.16 There was a suggestion that a compensation scheme for nurses for injuries received or stress following a violent incident at work should be established similar to that in place for gardai and prison officers.

Occupational Health

7.17 Many submissions asked the question "who cares for the carers?" There was a strong belief amongst nurses that there was a need for the provision of a more extensive occupational health service covering all health care facilities. While it was reported that many health employers have Employee Assistance Programmes, it was considered by some nurses that the existence of such schemes should be more widely communicated and their scope extended.

7.18 A submission from nurses working in an accident and emergency department described the importance of being facilitated to debrief each other particularly following critical incidents. Other submissions described situations where nurses having dealt with the consequences of a major accident were expected to continue with their work or go off duty without having the opportunity of discussing the experience with anyone. Nurses found this to be very traumatic and, it was submitted, this sometimes had adverse consequences either short-term or long-term.

7.19 Many nurses believed that there was a need for a professional confidential staff counselling service. The Commission learned that some health boards and voluntary hospitals had recently begun to offer a number of counselling sessions to nurses who might benefit from such a service.

7.20 Some submissions suggested the establishment of a health insurance scheme for nurses similar to that for ESB employees, prison officers and the gardai. Others suggested that nurses should generally be able to purchase prescribed medications for themselves and their families at a reduced rate in hospital pharmacies.

7.21 Concern was expressed about some of the physical structures within which health care services were provided to patients and within which nurses worked and the lack of facilities for nurses such as changing rooms and rest rooms. Dissatisfaction was expressed at the level of inspection under the Health and Safety Regulations carried out in the workplace. There was a call for full implementation of the legislation in this area.

Leave

7.22 An issue that arose in many submissions was that of annual leave entitlements. Many nurses submitted that the annual leave entitlements for nurses were much less than other professionals and clerical adminis- trative grades. There was no increase in annual leave with increased levels of responsibility which was seen as yet another disincentive to promotion. A comparison was made with clerical/administrative grades in the health service in particular, where for example, the annual leave for a Grade V Staff Officer was twenty eight days increasing to thirty days after three years in the post. In general, the annual leave for nurses at all levels was stated to be twenty four working days, with the exception of some superintendent public health nurses. It was suggested that extra annual leave should be commensurate with experience and grade. It was reported that privilege days for administrative grades in the health ser- vices (such as Good Friday and Christmas Eve) were not available to nursing staff.

7.23 Some public health nurses submitted that leave entitlements some- times varied between health boards and that this was inequitable.

7.24 Criticism was levelled at the method in which compassionate leave was granted. Many nurses complained that if a bereavement occurred on days off then those days were included as part of their compassionate leave. Nurses believed that this was unfair and uncaring. There was criticism of inconsistency in the interpretation of the Department of Health circular on compassionate leave.

Retirement Issues

7.25   While nurses acknowledged that the Public Service Pensions Commission would be examining in detail the whole issue of pensions/early retirement they believed that certain issues needed to be addressed.

7.26   Some nurses stated that their early retirement prospects were affected by the marriage bar which existed until the 1970s. Having to resign from a permanent post on marriage, meant that many nurses returned to work years later in a temporary capacity and therefore had limited superannuation entitlements.

7.27   It was pointed out that many nurses, on registration, went to work in nursing abroad for a variety of reasons. Some were obliged to seek employment or post-graduate experience or education; others welcomed the opportunity to travel and work abroad. Many nurses felt aggrieved that years of service in the nursing profession worked abroad, were not acknowledged for superannuation purposes in Ireland, making it very difficult for some nurses to have enough years to avail of early retirement schemes or to have a reasonable occupational pension on retirement.

7.28   Similarly, some nurses reported that if they had undertaken their training in a private hospital or worked in a private nursing home, those years were not reckonable for public service superannuation purposes.

7.29   Nurses believed that an inequity existed between the years of service required by those in the psychiatric service and the years required by other disciplines within the nursing profession. It was reported that following twenty years service as a psychiatric nurse, each year worked thereafter reckoned as two years service for superannuation purposes.

7.30   It was submitted that calculating a nurse's pension on the basis of gross earnings over the last three years can be unfair. It was said that this system:

  • places undue pressure on nurses to maximise week-end and
    night duty earnings over the last three years when they are less

able to cope with the demands of such rosters in this physically arduous and stressful profession; and

- undermines nurses flexibility in accepting roster changes which would have the effect of reducing their pension.

7.31 Some nurses submitted that pre-retirement programmes ought to be provided by their employing authority in preparation for retirement, where not already provided.

Other Issues

7.32 There were other issues relating to the employment of nurses which did not fit into any particular category. Many nurses were aggrieved that they were not paid for hand over time between shifts. Similarly, it was reported that if nurses were late going off duty, or returned from an ambulance call long after the end of their shift, they were repaid with time in lieu. Many nurses suggested that they should receive paid overtime or increased time in lieu for such situations.

7.33 The issue of acting up allowances featured in many submissions. It was suggested that if any grade "acted-up" in a position of responsibility then he or she should be paid an acting-up allowance for the actual time spent in that position. The current situation is that in the nursing profession a staff nurse must be in an acting-up position for one week prior to receiving an allowance (Department of Health Circular 32/59) whereas a ward sister must be acting-up for a month.

7.34 Criticism was also levelled at the practice of employing nurses, both permanent and temporary, in acting-up positions in vacant promotional posts for long periods. Many nurses suggested that such posts ought to be filled without delay.

7.35 As stated earlier many nurses work outside Ireland for periods following their registration. Some complained that on returning to Ireland, having acquired many years experience abroad they were placed on the incremental scale with no recognition of the experience gained in nursing outside the country.

7.36 It was reported by many nurses employed in hospitals with a school of nursing and in public health nursing that preceptor nurses were not recognised for their contribution to nurse education. Preceptor nurses have responsibility for supervising and helping students to attain their learning objectives in clinical environments. Preceptor nurses believed that the extra responsibility which they held ought to be duly rewarded.

7.37   A submission was received from phlebotomists, the majority of whom are nurses, in which they draw attention to the disparity of terms and conditions of employment throughout the country.

7.38   The issue of meal times was raised in a number of submissions. Some nurses submitted that mealtimes ought to be included in the rostered hours. It was claimed by some nurses that when on night duty, one hour meal breaks were deducted from the total hours on duty. This was considered to be unfair as nurses could not leave the hospital during this time. It was also submitted that some nurses who were part of cardiac arrest teams often had to hold the bleep and often had meals interrupted to answer an emergency call.

References

An Bord Altranais (1988) *The Code of Professional Conduct for Each Nurse and Midwife*, Dublin: An Bord Altranais.

An Bord Altranais (1994) *The Future of Nurse Education and Training in Ireland*, Dublin: An Bord Altranais.

An Bord Altranais (1997) *Continuing Professional Education for Nurses in Ireland: A Framework*, Dublin: An Bord Altranais.

An Bord Altranais (1997) *Guidance to Nurses and Midwives on the Administration of Medical Preparations*, 4th ed. Dublin: An Bord Altranais.

Department of Health (1966) *Commission of Enquiry on Mental Illness: Report*, Dublin: Stationery Office.

Department of Health (1980) *Working Party on General Nursing: Report*, Dublin: Stationery Office.

Department of Health (1984) *The Psychiatric Services: Planning for the Future*, Dublin: Stationery Office.

Department of Health (1992) *Green Paper on Mental Health*, Dublin: Stationery Office.

Department of Health (1994) *Shaping a Healthier Future*, Dublin: Stationery Office.

71

Department of Health (1996) *A Management Development Strategy for the Health and Personal Social Services in Ireland,* Dublin: Stationery Office.

Henderson V. (1960) *Basic Principles of Care,* London: International Council of Nurses.

O'Connor P. (1996) Organisational Culture as a Barrier to Womens Promotion, *Economic and Social Review,* 27(3), pp 205-234.

United Kingdom Central Council for Nursing, Midwifery and Health Visiting (1992) *The Scope of Professional Practice,* London: UKCC, pp 6-8.

The International Council of Nurses (1987) *Definition approved by the Council of National Representatives,* Geneva: ICN.

APPENDIX

List of written submissions
received by the
Commission on Nursing

Appendix

List of Submissions Received

1. Ms. Liz Sheridan
   Co. Sligo

2. A McCarthy
   Co. Cork

3. Ms. Noreen Roche
   Co. Tipperary

4. Ms. Catherine Hayes
   London

5. Anonymous Letter

6. Nurses
   St. Joseph's Hospital
   Castletownbere
   Co. Cork

7. Mr. Martin Clancy
   Co. Clare

8. Ms. Kay Shine
   Co. Louth

9. Ms. Clare Kelly
   National Children's Hospital
   Dublin 2

10. Staff Nurses
    Macroom District Hospital

11. Mr. Gearoid Donnchadha
    Co. Wicklow

12. Assistant Nurses
    St. John of God Brothers
    Co. Louth

13. Ms. Maureen Gaughran
    Co. Louth

14. Nursing Staff
    St. Camillus' Hospital
    Limerick

15. Ms. Breda Brady
    Dublin 2

16. Ms. Claire Nee

17. Mr. Malachy Feely
    Co. Meath

18. Ms. Orla Ryan
    Dublin 18

19. Mr. John O'Neill
    Co. Wexford

20. Ms. Catherine Hogan
    Dublin 14

21. Ms. Erica Shipman
    Co. Dublin

22. Mrs. Kathleen Ensko
    Co. Mayo

23. "A Service without Walls" —
    An Analysis of Public Health
    Nursing in 1994

24. Mr. Martin Hewitt
    Co. Kildare

25. Mrs. Anne Forde
    Co. Offaly

26. Ms. Margaret Walshe
    Dublin 15

27. Ms. Sheila O'Connor
    Co. Cork

28. Public Health Nurses
    in North Kerry

29. Staff Working in 3 Psychiatric
    Day Centres
    Eastern Health Board

30. Public Health Nurses
    Dublin 9

31. Ms. Clara Ni Ghiolla
    Belfast

32. Mr. Donal O'Sullivan
    & Ms. Winifred Leonard
    Dublin 7

33. Mr. Liam Gormley
    Co. Wicklow

34. Hospital Pharmacists' Association
    Ireland

35. Mr. Jimmy Stenson
    Co. Westmeath

36. M Finlay
    Co. Laois

37. Anonymous

38. Ms. Teresa Lynch
    Co. Laois

39. Anonymous

40. Ms. Brigid O'Connor
    Co. Cork

41. Ms. Ursula Cafferty
    Co. Westmeath

42. Ms. Betty Foley
    Co. Kerry

43. Ms. Mary Kelly
    Co. Kerry

44. Ms. Mary Teresa Devane
    Co. Kerry

45. Nursing Administration
    General Hospital Tullamore

46. Ms. Marie Conlon
    Co. Laois

47. Temporary Nursing Staff
    Co. Laois

48. Representation of Staff
    from a Day Activity Centre
    for People with Learning
    Disabilities in Dublin

49. Enrolled Nurses
    Cherry Orchard Hospital

50. Institute of Guidance Counsellors
    North Eastern Branch
    Co. Monaghan

51. Ms. Ann Winters
    Co. Mayo

52. Ms. Colette Costello
    Limerick

53. Ms. Eithne O'Reilly Gulry
    Cavan

54. Ms. Catherine Hanrahan
    Limerick

55. Ms. Claire Crowe
    Dublin 12

56. Mr. Brian Denham
    Dublin 4

57. Irish Association of Nursing in
    Aids Care (IANAC)

58. Ms. Anne McElligott
    Co. Kerry

59. Ms. Helen Duffy
    Co. Dublin

60. Ms. Margaret Cotter
Co. Cork

61. Ms. Eileen Hennigan
Co. Dublin

62. Ms. Fionnuala O'Gorman
Cork

63. Detoxification Unit
Beaumont Hospital

64. Home Care Management Team
From Swords & Balbriggan
Co. Dublin

65. Mr. Albert Murphy
Waterford

66. Ms. Mary Thornton
Co. Clare

67. Ms. Patricia Lynch Manning
Co. Cork

68. Ms. Bernadette Walker
Co. Westmeath

69. Ms. Veronica Gibbons
Co. Westmeath

70. Ms. Rose Conlon
Co. Westmeath

71. Ms. Pauline Woods
Co. Louth

72. Longford Public Health Nurses

73. Mrs. Phil Yourell
Co. Westmeath

74. Mrs. Theresa Maguire
Dublin 9

75. Nurse Tutors
Co. Donegal

76. Mr. Tony Barden
Waterford

77. Pat O'Neill
Waterford

78. Mr. Tom Care
Dublin 14

79. Sunbeam House Services
Co. Wicklow

80. Ms. Valarie Small
Dublin 8

81. Midwifery Tutors
National Maternity Hospital

82. Mr. William Cronin
Cork

83. Senior Public Health Nurses
South Eastern Health Board

84. Ms. Geraldine Darcy
Limerick

85. Night Sisters
COPE Foundation
Cork

86. Ms. Nora Quill
Co. Cork

87. Student Midwives
Co. Cork

88. Ms. Monica M Collins
Co. Offaly

89. Nursing Staff Involved in
Care of the Elderly
Midland Health Board

90. Ms. Mary Dunne
Co. Offaly

91. Acute Pain Service
Beaumont Hospital

92. Nursing Advisory Forum of the
Irish Association for Palliative
Care

93. Nurses/Addiction Counsellors
Western Health Board

94. Mr. Joe Faulkner
Sligo General Hospital

95. Ms. Catherine O'Sullivan
Cork

96. Theatre Department
Waterford Regional Hospital

97. Nursing Staff
St. Brendan's Home
Co. Galway

98. Staff Nurses
Brothers of Charity Services
Boyle

99. Ms. Ann Sharkey
Co. Louth

100. Ms. Sheila O'Reilly
Cork

101. Nurse Manager Branch
Psychiatric Nurses Association

102. Ms. Philomena Stynes
Co. Dublin

103. Unit Nurse Officers/Services
Managers
Sligo General Hospital

104. Ms. Margo Topham
Cork

105. Nurse Tutors
Letterkenny

106. Nurses from
Carrigoran Nursing Home
Co. Clare

107. Ms. Mary Kelly
Co. Offaly

108. Ms. Maureen Crowley
Co. Cork

109. Nursing Administrator Sisters
in Beaumont Hospital in Charge
of Out of Hours Services

110. Community Psychiatric Nurses
Sligo

111. Mr. Henry Abbott
Co. Westmeath

112. Staff from the Outpatient
Department
St. John's Hospital
Limerick

113. Phil Murphy
Co. Cork

114. Community Nurses working
within Early Childhood Services
in the Brothers of Charity in
Galway and Roscommon

115. Anonymous

116. J Leahy
Kilkenny

117. Ms. Nora Garahy
Co. Offaly

118. First Floor Staff Nurses
St. John's Hospital
Limerick

119. Ms. Judith Chavasse
Dublin 14

120. Infection Control
NursesAssociation (Irish Group)

121. Nurses working in the
Eastern Health Board's
Aids/Drugs Services

122. The Donegal Practice Nurses

123. Psychiatric Nurses with Family
Therapy Qualifications from
North Western Health Board

124. Community Nursing Group
Area 7 Psychiatric Services
Eastern Health Board

125. Community Psychiatric Nurses in
the Roscommon Psychiatric Service

126. Sligo Association of Critical
Care Nurses (S.A.C.C.N.)

127. Ms. M O'Flynn
Co. Cork

128. Ms. Elaine O'Dwyer
Waterford Regional Hospital

129. Ms. Frances McHugh
Sligo General Hospital

130. Public Health Nurses
Institute of Community
Health Nursing
Longford/Westmeath Branch

131. Representative Group
of Nurses working in
New and Developing
Community Mental
Health Projects in the
Mayo Psychiatric Service

132. INO Members
District Hospital
Listowel

133. 3rd Year Students (1994 Intake)
Letterkenny General Hospital

134. Nurses from
COPE Foundation
Cork

135. Ms. Mary Syron
Co. Galway

136. Ms. Helen Plunkett
Limerick

137. Anonymous

138. Ms. Anna O'Brien
Cork

139. Anonymous

140. Regional Technical Colleges
Nurses

141. Mr. Eugene Caulfield
North Eastern Health Board

142. Ms. Eilis Fullam
Co. Kildare

143. Ms. Deirdre Clarke
Dublin 5

144. Ms. Rita Moloney
Co. Kildare

145. L Kelly
Dublin 14

146. Ms. Jane Donohue
Co. Meath

147. Public Health Nurses
Tuam

148. Ms. Mary Glennon
Co. Kildare

149. Ward Sisters employed by
COPE Foundation
Cork

150. Nurses engaged in the
Service for the Elderly at
Cork University/St. Finbarr's
Hospitals

151. Senior Public Health Nurses
Institute of Community
Health Nursing

152. Psychiatric Nurse Managers
in the Cork Area

153. Clinical Nurse Specialist Group
in Cystic Fibrosis in Ireland

154. Midwifery Staff
National Maternity Hospital

155. Nursing Staff
Portiuncula Hospital
Galway

156. Mr. Lawrence Cunningham
Co. Westmeath

157. Ms. Eileen Fitzgerald
Kilkenny

158. Ms. Margaret O'Connell
Waterford

159. Ms. Bridget Ryan
Co. Cork

160. Staff from the
Intensive Care Unit
Wexford General Hospital

161. Ms. Patricia F Harte
Sligo General Hospital

162. The Nurses of
St. Columbanus Home
Killarney

163. Ms. Mary Burke
Co. Tipperary

164. Irish Association of Addiction
Counsellors
Midland Health Board Regional
Group

165. Mr. Michael O'Keeffe
Co. Cork

166. Ms. Mary Mulvihill
Co. Tipperary

167. Community Psychiatric Nurses
East Galway Psychiatric Services

168. Ms. Marie McCarthy
Co. Cork

169. Ms. Marion Moriarty
Limerick

170. Ms. Myriam Leahy
Co. Cork

171. Anonymous

172. Irish Nursing Research Interest
Group

173. Matrons' of the Geriatric
Hospitals of the South East Region

174. Nursing Officers in the
Mayo Psychiatric Services

175. Staff Nurses
Coronary Care Unit
Beaumont Hospital

176. Ms. Rita Smith
Dublin 16

177. Ms. Anne Fox
Dublin 9

178. Ms. Maura O'Brien
Co. Tipperary

179. Ms. Frances Kennedy
Co. Tipperary

180. Ms. Moya Carroll
Cavan

181. Community Psychiatric
Nurses from the South Eastern
Health Board

182. Diabetes Nurses
Beaumont Hospital

183. Ms. Margaret McCarthy
Limerick Regional Hospital

184. Senior Public Health Nurses
Co. Kerry

185. Mr. Jim Thomas
Co. Mayo

186. Irish Association of Critical
Care Nurses

187. St. Colman's Hospital
Co. Wicklow

188. Members of Institute of
Community Health Nursing

189. Generic Community Psychiatric
Nurses in the Donegal Area of the
North Western Health Board

190. Senior Nurse Managers
South Eastern Health Board

191. Ms. Deirdre Kavanagh
& Ms. Maura Colgan
Eastern Health Board

192. Nurse Tutors
School of Nursing
Sligo

193. Ms. Ita Tighe
Dublin 3

194. The Cognitive Behavioural
     Psychotherapists
     North Western Health Board

195. Community Psychiatric Clinical
     Nurse Specialists in Addiction in
     the Donegal Area of the
     North Western Health Board

196. Association of Administrative
     Psychiatric Nurses (AAPN)

197. Ms. Marianne Doran
     Beaumont Hospital

198. Staff Nurses
     Top Floor
     St. John's Hospital
     Limerick

199. Public Health Nurses
     Mid-Western Health Board

200. Liver Transplant Co-ordinators
     St. Vincent's Hospital
     Dublin 4

201. Nursing Officer Group (Psych)
     St. Loman's Hospital
     Dublin 20

202. Education Committee
     St. Loman's Hospital
     Dublin 20

203. Public Health Nurses
     Class 96/97
     University College Dublin

204. Course Co-ordinators
     St. Vincent's/Mater Hospitals

205. Ms. Sandy Mason
     Co. Louth

206. Ms. Noreen Keane
     Dublin 9

207. Ms. Eileen McKenna
     Co. Kerry

208. Ms. Sinead Hanafin
     University College Cork

209. Mr. Mark Monahan
     Dublin 9

210. Ms. Martina Kehoe
     Waterford Regional Hospital

211. Ms. Joan Phyllis Kirwan
     Waterford Regional Hospital

212. Ms. Susan O'Donoghue
     Waterford Regional Hospital

213. Dr. Colin Buckley
     Waterford Regional Hospital

214. Ms. Avril O'Leary
     Dublin 9

215. Mr. Jim Brosnan
     Dublin 20

216. Nurse Members
     attached to Clondalkin
     and Tallaght Mental
     Health Services from
     St. Loman's Hospital
     Dublin 20

217. Mr. Malachy Nugent
     Dublin 7

218. Ms. Mary Tynan

219. Theatre Nursing Staff
     Beaumont Hospital

220. Ms. Siobhan Ni Scanaill
     & Ms. Jane Leavy
     Dublin 8

221. Members of the Irish Association
     of Operating Theatre
     Superintendents/Managers

222. Director and Family Development
     Nurses of the Community
     Mothers Programme
     Eastern Health Board

223. Saville & Holdsworth
     University of Limerick

224. Nurse Education Committee
Sligo General Hospital

225. Diabetes Nurse Specialist Group
St. Vincent's Hospital
Dublin 4

226. Department of Community
Psychiatric Nursing
St. Patrick's Hospital
Dublin 8

227. Community RGN's
Dublin 14

228. Renal Unit
Sligo General Hospital

229. Ms. Bernie Morrisroe
Sligo General Hospital

230. Ms. Mary Gillan
Sligo General Hospital

231. Ms. Madeleine Munnelly
Sligo General Hospital

232. L Ruttledge
Sligo General Hospital

233. Ms. Noreen O'Sullivan
Sligo General Hospital

234. Ms. Mary Flatley
Sligo General Hospital

235. Ms. Karen Reynolds
Sligo General Hospital

236. Ms. Margaret Towey
Sligo General Hospital

237. G O'Brien
Sligo General Hospital

238. Ms. Karen E Fagan
Sligo General Hospital

239. Ms. Maureen Campbell
Sligo General Hospital

240. Ms. Rosemary Irwin
Sligo General Hospital

241. Ms. Ciara Swayelen
Sligo General Hospital

242. Staff Nurses working in the
Field of Learning Disabilities
Cork

243. Ms. Imelda B McCarthy
Cork

244. Ms. Joan Phelan

245. Midwifery Staff
Rotunda Hospital

246. Public Health Nurses
Southern Health Board

247. Ms. Margaret Freeney
Limerick

248. Public Health Nurses
Roscommon Area

249. Junior Ward Sisters
Intensive Care Unit
Beaumont Hospital

250. Staff Nurses
Intensive Care Unit
Beaumont Hospital

251. Ms. Sheila Fitzgerald
Dublin 10

252. Ms. Mary Villiers
Co. Cork

253. Ms. Elizabeth Doyle
Dublin 15

254. Ms. Patricia Campbell
Co. Meath

255. Public Health Nurses/Addiction
Counsellors
Eastern Health Board

256. Nursing Staff
Ard Aoibhinn Centre
Wexford

257. Lifford Community Hospital

258. Dual Qualified Registered
Psychiatric and Registered
General Nurses
Tralee General Hospital

259. Ms. Caroline Dolan
& Ms. Catherine Croffy
Co. Galway

260. Terry Hayes
Co. Waterford

261. University College Galway

262. Theatre Staff
Lourdes Orthopaedic Hospital
Kilkenny

263. Nursing Staff
Lourdes Orthopaedic Hospital
Kilkenny

264. INO Midwife Members
The Coombe Hospital
Dublin 8

265. Ms. Maureen Lynn/
Ms. Jacqueline Egan
St. James's Hospital

266. St. Vincent's Hospital
Fairview
Dublin 3

267. Health Counsel
Dublin 3

268. Nursing Staff
St. Patrick's Ward
Beaumont Hospital

269. Ms. Angela Lally
Dublin Dental Hospital

270. Health Sciences Group
of the Library Association
of Ireland

271. Ms. Margaret O'Brien
Dublin 6

272. Ms. Anne Murphy
Meath Hospital
& Ms. Anna Craig
National Children's Hospital

273. Irish Pharmaceutical Union

274. Ms. Sandra Keating
Co. Offaly

275. Ms. Mary Riordan
Dublin 2

276. Irish Business and Employers
Confederation

277. Tutorial Staff
School of Nursing
Mater Hospital

278. Liaison Nurses Forum
Our Lady's Hospital for Sick
Children
Crumlin

279. The Children's Hospital
Temple Street

280. Anonymous

281. Nurses from Phlebotomy,
Urodynamics and Outpatient
Departments
Beaumont Hospital

282. Ms. Edwina O'Keeffe
Kilkenny

283. Occupational Health Department
Waterford Regional Hospital

284. Nursing Staff
St. Patrick's Geriatric Hospital
Cashel
Co. Tipperary

285. National Nursing Sisters
Association

286. Midwives in Ultrasonography
Rotunda Hospital

287. Maternity Unit
Letterkenny General Hospital

288. Cork Voluntary Hospitals
School of Nursing

289. Ms. Eileen Cullen
& Ms. Eilis Breen

290. Ms. Margaret McGillycuddy
Wexford

291. Female Surgical
St. Luke's General Hospital
Kilkenny

292. Ms. Una Webster
Co. Cork

293. Mr. Sean McCarty
Waterford

294. Ms. Marie Healy
Co. Cork

295. RNMH's working in
the community in Cork and Kerry

296. Ms. Maureen Cahill
Co. Cork

297. Ms. Maura Fagan
Co. Louth

298. Matrons/Directors of Nursing
Care of the Elderly Service
North Eastern Health Board

299. Area Co-ordinators
Care of the Elderly
North Eastern Health Board

300. The Irish Matrons' Association

301. Psychiatric Nurses
Area 7 Psychiatric Services
Eastern Health Board

302. The National Rehabilitation
Hospital
Dun Laoghaire

303. A Fitzsimons
Royal Victoria Eye and Ear
Hospital
Dublin 2

304. Ms. Breda Jones
Dublin 3

305. Institute of Public Administration

306. Mrs. Eileen Maher
& Ms. Wendy Fair

St. Luke's Hospital
Dublin 6

307. Faculty of Health Sciences
Trinity College Dublin

308. Union of Students in Ireland

309. M W Quigley
Galway

310. Domiciliary Midwives and
Home Births in Ireland

311. National Rehabilitation Board

312. Association of Nurse Teachers

313. Mr. John Fitzpatrick
Co. Kildare

314. Ms. Patricia Fitzpatrick
Co. Kildare

315. Ward Sister Association
St. Finbarr's Hospital
Cork

316. Ms. Jean Harrison
North Eastern Health Board

317. Ward Sisters
St. Luke's Hospital
Kilkenny

318. Public Health Nurses
Area 2
Eastern Health Board

319. Mr. Geoff Day
North Eastern Health Board

320. Ms. Jane Boyle
Donegal

321. Ms. Clare O'Herlihy
Cork

322. Nurses from St. Anne's Hospital
Dublin 6

323. National Neurosurgical Unit
Beaumont Hospital

324. The Board
Faculty of Nursing
Royal College of Surgeons

325. Outreach Counsellors
working in the Aids/Drugs
Service of the
Eastern Health Board

326. Nursing Staff of the Hospital
Adelaide and Meath
incorporating the
National Children's Hospital

327. Nursing Staff
St. Loman's Hospital
Mullingar

328. Nursing School
National Children's Hospital
Harcourt Street

329. Nursing Staff of the
National Children's Hospital
Harcourt Street

330. Cardiac Catheterization
Laboratory
St. James's Hospital

331. Radiology Staff Nurses
St. James's Hospital

332. Behaviour Nurse
Psychotherapists from
the Eastern Region

333. Ms. Miriam McCarthy
Co. Wicklow

334. B N Brown
Galway

335. National Senior Public
Health Nurses

336. Senior Public Health Nurses of
the Eastern Health Board

337. The Irish Association for Nurses in
Oncology

338. Ms. Joan Kelly
Irish Cancer Society

339. Midwives
Our Lady of Lourdes Hospital
Drogheda

340. Nursing and Midwifery Staff
Our Lady of Lourdes Hospital
Drogheda

341. Nurse Tutors
School of Nursing
Beaumont Hospital

342. Mr. Martin Connor
& Mr. John McTiernan
Community Care Area 8
Eastern Health Board

343. Nursing Administration and
Nursing Staff
St. Vincent's Hospital
Co. Laois

344. Ms. Lorna Kelleher
Cork

345. The Nurse Teachers
The School of Nursing
St. Vincent's Hospital
Elm Park
Dublin 4

346. Miss J Bartley
Beaumont Hospital

347. Psychiatric Nurse
Managers in the Cork area

348. Irish Registered Nursing
Homes Association

349. Department of Nursing
St. Vincent's Hospital
Elm Park
Dublin 4

350. Ms. Joan Moyles
Co. Mayo

351. The National Superintendent
Public Health Nurses Group

352. Ms. Joan Murray
Beaumont Hospital

353. Association of Family Planning
Nurses Ireland

354. Dr. Aine O'Sullivan
Cavan

355. Staff Nurses
COPE Foundation
Hollyhill
Cork

356. Senior Nurse Managers
St. Finbarr's Hospital
Cork

357. Public Health Students
University College Cork

358. Nursing Staff
Medical Floor
St. Luke's Hospital
Kilkenny

359. Ms. Margaret Maguire
Sligo General Hospital

360. Mr. John McNally
Monaghan

361. St. Bridget's Hospital
Carrick-on-Suir
Co. Tipperary

362. Ms. Noreen Cremin
Co. Kerry

363. Community Psychiatric Nurses
Community Care Area 8
Eastern Health Board

364. Board and Staff of
Cheeverstown House Limited
Templeogue
Dublin 6W

365. Ms. Irene O'Mahony
& Ms. Karen Kelleher
University College Cork

366. Ms. Mary Burke
Co. Offaly

367. Ms. Ciara Davin
Dublin 4

368. Group of West Cork
Public Health Nurses

369. Nursing Staff
St. John's Community Hospital
Sligo

370. Ms. Breda O'Donoghue
Co. Cork

371. Staff from
St. Patrick's Hospital
Cashel
Co. Tipperary

372. Ms. Brigid Caldwell
Co. Longford

373. Ms. Norma Kissane
Co. Kerry

374. Anonymous

375. Ms. Stephanie Ryan
Co. Tipperary

376. Ms. Mary Cullinan
Co. Offaly

377. Ms. Ann Cahalane
Co. Cork

378. Ms. Marion Barnes
Co. Kerry

379. Mr. David Healy
Co. Cork

380. Ms. Kathryn Healy
Co. Cork

381. Ms. Sarah A Lawless
Co. Mayo

382. Ms. Helen P McLoughlin
Co. Offaly

383. Ms. Fiona Robins-Claffey
Co. Offaly

384. Ms. Eileen O'Heney
Co. Westmeath

385. Ms. Peggy Murtagh
Co. Westmeath

386. Nurses
Eye Department
Waterford Regional Hospital

387. Ms. Elizabeth Cuddy Devine
Roscommon

388. Ms. Nuala Cashlin
Letterkenny General Hospital
& Ms. Ann Monaghan
Sligo General Hospital

389. Ms. Jill Anthony
Waterford Regional Hospital

390. Accident & Emergency Sisters
Beaumont Hospital

391. Geriatric Section
Sacred Heart Hospital
Castlebar

392. Ms. Maura Walsh
Waterford Regional Hospital

393. Senior Nurse Managers
Donegal Mental Health Services

394. Ward Sisters
& Junior Ward Sisters
Brothers of Charity
Co. Roscommon Services

395. Ward Sisters
Sligo General Hospital

396. Registered Nurses in Mental
Handicap
St. Vincent's Centre
Co. Limerick

397. Rescue Trust

398. Degree Nurses Association

399. Dermatologist Nurses
City of Dublin Skin and Cancer
Hospital
Dublin 2

400. Working Group
National Association for the
Mentally Handicapped of Ireland

401. Stoma Care Department
Baggot Street Community Hospital

402. October 1996 intake of Student
Nurses at Sligo General Hospital

403. Registered General Nurses in
Community Care Area 4
who are Members of IMPACT

404. Mr. Paul Gallagher
Dublin 9

405. Ms. Bernadette Carpenter
Co. Dublin

406. Nursing Staff
Heath County Infirmary
Navan

407. Ms. Maria M Murphy
Cork

408. Ms. Ann Mason
Cork

409. Ms. Triona Leyden
Co. Sligo

410. Anonymous

411. Ms. Dolores Gavin Doyle
Co. Cork

412. Ms. Ellen Manny
Co. Westmeath

413. St. Luke's Hospital
Kilkenny

414. Ms. Eleanor O'Connor
Cork

415. Anonymous

416. Ms. Kathleen McGovern
Sligo

417. Unit Directors of the
Galway County Association
for Mentally Handicapped
Children

418. Ms. Margaret Dillon
Limerick

419. Association of Behaviour Therapists in Services for People with Learning Disabilities

420. Ms. Claire Gough
Co. Mayo

421. SIPTU Members
Mayo Health Services

422. Bed Managers Group
St. James's Hospital

423. St. Brigid's CPN Group
Co. Louth

424. Louth/Meath Family Therapy Service

425. Ms. Geraldine Hoyne
Co. Tipperary

426. Mr. Eugene McCormack
Co. Mayo

427. Clinical Placement Co-ordinators
Beaumont Hospital

428. Ms. Catherine Lavin
& Ms. Mary O'Dowd
Co. Mayo

429. Tutorial Staff
St. Louise's School of Nursing
St. Joseph's Hospital
Dublin 15

430. Ward Sisters
Mater Misericordiae Hospital

431. Nursing Sisters
University College Hospital
Galway

432. Nurses
University College Hospital
Galway

433. Ms. Imelda Tobin
Co. Cork

434. Department of Nursing Studies
University College Dublin

435. Ms. Maureen Flynn
Dublin 4

436. Nursing Staff
Our Lady's Hospital for Sick Children
Crumlin

437. Nurse Managers Association (Mental Handicap)

438. Association of Nurses in Radiology

439. Co-ordinators for Continuing Education in three Health Board Areas

440. Ms. Catherine Quinn
Limerick

441. Mr. Oliver O'Connor
Cavan

442. Ms. Margaret Fleming
Monaghan

443. Ms. Imelda Connolly O'Connor
Co. Limerick

444. My. Lynda Moore
Cork

445. Ms. Mary Harvey
Co. Clare

446. Education Committee
Letterkenny General Hospital

447. Pat Monaghan
Galway

448. Nursing Officers and Deputy Nursing Officers
St. Dympna's Hospital
Carlow

449. Computer Nurse Co-ordinators
Meath and Adelaide Hospitals

450. Ms. Mary Harte
Sligo General Hospital

451. The Irish Innovative Nurse Management Network

452. Ms. Mary Kearney
Co. Galway

453. Ms. Maria McInerney
Limerick

454. Mr. Michael Gilligan,
Mr. Peadar Ryan
& Mr. Eugene McCormack

455. INO Members
St. John's Hospital
Enniscorthy

456. Ms. Marian Keely
Co. Tipperary

457. Ms. Sheila Reilly
Co. Tipperary

458. Ward Sisters
University College Hospital
Galway

459. Chief Nursing Officer Group
(Psychiatric Service)
Eastern Health Board

460. Nursing Staff
University College Hospital
Galway

461. Public Health Nurses
in Community Care Area 5
Eastern Health Board

462. Ms. Veronica Mee
Co. Dublin

463. Dr. Colette Halpin
on behalf of Child Psychiatrists
in Ireland

464. Nurse Management
Limerick Regional Hospital

465. Mr. David Kieran
Co. Tipperary

466. Ms. Rita Higgins
Cavan

467. Educational Committee
Mallow General Hospital

468. Ms. Kathleen Seaver
Kilkenny

469. Cork and Kerry Nurse
Education Committee

470. Louth/Meath Hospital Group

471. Ms. Mary Rogers
Galway

472. Ms. Anne O'Byrne
Co. Wicklow

473. St. Angela's College of Education
Sligo

474. Professor John Carroll
Dublin City University

475. Public Health Nurses
in the Gorey Area
Co. Wexford

476. Ms. Ita Healy
Co. Meath

477. Ms. Patricia Barrett
Co. Mayo

478. Mr. John Fennessy
Co. Tipperary

479. Night Superintendents
St. James's Hospital

480. Council of the Pharmaceutical
Society of Ireland

481. Public Health Nurses
Working Group
Cavan

482. Mr. John Murray
Waterford

483. Ms. Fiona McGrath
Dublin 7

484. Ms. Mary Doyle
Wexford General Hospital

485. Ms. Nora Kane
Waterford Regional Hospital

486. Ms. Mary Heffernan
Co. Limerick

487. Ms. Anne Costigan
Tipperary

488. Ms. Ann Gallagher
Co. Donegal

489. Ms. Joan Meaney
Limerick

490. Ms. Anne Gilbourne
Limerick Regional Hospital

491. Ms. Brigid Burke
Co. Waterford

492. Dialysis Unit
Letterkenny General Hospital

493. Nursing Officers & Deputy
Nursing Officers
St. Brigid's Hospital
Ballinasloe

494. Radiology/Cardiology Nurses
University College Hospital
Cork

495. Mr. Jim Brett
Co. Mayo

496. Ward Sisters & Staff Nurses
St. Nessan's Regional
Orthopaedic Hospital
Croom

497. Mr. Edmond McManamon
Co. Westmeath

498. Mr. Padraic Noone
Co. Galway

499. Ms. Mary Lyons
& Ms. Eileen Higgins
Co. Roscommon

500. Sisters of La Sagesse Services
Cregg House
Sligo

501. Nursing Staff
Intensive Care Unit
University College Hospital
Galway

502. Ms. Myra O'Brien
Co. Roscommon

503. Anonymous

504. Anonymous

505. Ms. Trina Nolan
Galway

506. Ms. Geraldine Flynn
Wexford General Hospital

507. Phil Mahony
Kilkenny

508. Mr. Barry Walsh
Carlow

509. Ms. Julia B Moloney
Co. Galway

510. State Enrolled Nurses working in
Hospitals in the Midlands

511. Ms. Sarah White
Co. Dublin

512. Mr. Peter Ledden
Dublin 3

513. Nursing Practice Development
Co-ordinators

514. Ms. Teresa Walsh
Galway

515. Ms. Deirdre Harrington
Co. Roscommon

516. Matrons of the Eastern Health
Board

517. Director of Nursing
and Nursing Staff
St. James's Hospital

518. Ms. Marie Molan
Co. Tipperary

519. Ward Sisters
General Hospital
Naas

520. Ms. Anne Cleary

521. Ms. Maeve Hanley,
Ms. Maureen Merne
& Ms. Teresa Murphy
Carlow

522. Ms. Anne Clarke
Co. Wicklow

523. Ms. Mary Durkin
Sligo General Hospital

524. Mr. P Finnegan
Co. Mayo

525. Ms. Sheena Faulkner

526. Ms. Olive Veerkamp
Co. Louth

527. Ms. Fiona Byrne

528. D Coyle
Co. Louth

529. Ms. Geraldine O'Reilly
Co. Louth

530. Ms. Ann McKenna
Co. Louth

531. Ms. Lorraine Glynn
Co. Louth

532. Ms. Antoinette Martin
Co. Louth

533. Ms. Geraldine Roche
Co. Louth

534. Lee Byrne
Co. Louth

535. Ms. Marian Spelman
Co. Louth

536. Ms. Aine McKenny
Co. Louth

537. Ms. Margaret Rowan
Co. Louth

538. Ms. Mary Cuthbert
Co. Louth

539. Ms. Stephanie Brennan
Co. Louth

540. Anonymous

541. Ms. Muriel Dawe

542. Ms. Laura Breen
Co. Louth

543. Ms. Mary Courtney McDonnell
Co. Louth

544. Ms. Amanda Lavery
Co. Louth

545. Ms. Cathy Baylon
Co. Louth

546. Health and Safety Authority

547. Midwives Association of Ireland

548. Ms. Katherine Hogan
Waterford Regional Hospital

549. Sr. Nora Leonard
Co. Waterford

550. Ms. Alice O'Connor
Waterford

551. Mr. Eugene Cadden
Dublin 7

552. Ms. Margaret McCafferty
Sligo General Hospital

553. St. Louise's School of Nursing
in conjunction with Nurse
Practitioners from
St. Joseph's Hospital
Dublin 15

554. Ms. Brigid Barron
Co. Clare

555. Roscommon County Hospital

556. Ms. Lillian O'Connor
Co. Limerick

557. Ms. Deirdre Carroll
Co. Limerick

558. Mr. Gerard O'Neill
Waterford

559. School of Nursing
Waterford Regional Hospital

560. A Twomey
Waterford

561. The Federation of Voluntary
Bodies
Galway Association

562. Mr. Willie Hackett& Mr. Paul
Maher

563. National University of Ireland
Nursing Studies Department

564. Ward Sisters
Tralee General Hospital

565. Ms. Alice Cox
Carlow

566. Phlebotomists Association of
Ireland

567. Nursing Staff
St. Mary's Hospital
Dublin 20

568. Leslie Proudfoot
Dublin 4

569. Sr. Mary Morrisroe
Limerick

570. Ms. Elizabeth Heffernan
Co. Kerry

571. SIPTU Branch
St. Canice's Hospital
Kilkenny

572. Ms. Hannah O'Leary
Co. Tipperary

573. Ms. Cathy Kinsella
Kilkenny

574. Tutorial Staff
School of Nursing
Limerick Regional Hospital

575. Hospitaller Order of
Saint John of God
Co. Dublin

576. Ms. Angela Clarke
Co. Louth

577. Mid-Western Branch
Irish Nursing Research
Interest Group

578. Nurse Managers/Matrons
Western Health Board Area

579. Ms. Annette Gee
Waterford Regional Hospital

580. The Nursing Staff of the Eastern
Health Board
Child Psychiatric Services

581. Age and Opportunity Marino
Institute of Education
Dublin 9

582. Midwives
St. Finbarr's Hospital
Cork

583. Irish Health Services
Management Institute

584. Public Health Nurses
Community Care Area 4
Eastern Health Board

585. Ms. Bridget Kinsella
Co. Wicklow

586. Anonymous

587. Ward Attendants
Limerick Regional Hospital

588. Anonymous

589. Ms. Mary E Doherty
Co. Donegal

590. Public Health Nurses
New Ross Area

591. Ms. Mary Keogh
Carlow/Kilkenny

592. South Tipperary Nursing
Branch SIPTU

593. Ms. Teresa O'Brien
Co. Tipperary

594. Ms. Bridie O'Connor
Co. Galway

595. Ms. Mary Cronin
& Ms. Elke Hasner

596. Ms. Mary Killeen McCarthy
Co. Clare

597. Irish Practice Nurses Association

598. Night Superintendents
North Eastern Health Board

599. Clinical Nurse Specialists
Eastern Health Board

600. Ms. Maura Ryan
Limerick

601. Mr. Michael O'Sullivan
Southern Health Board

602. Sr. Celestine
Co. Cork

603. Degree Nurses
Class of 1996
University College Cork

604. Matrons in Care of the Elderly
Mid-Western Health Board Area

605. Ms. Geraldine Freeman
Co. Galway

606. Public Health Nurses
Dingle Area

607. Care of the Elderly Day Hospital

608. School of Nursing
Tralee General Hospital

609. Staff Nurses
Tralee General Hospital

610. Public Health Nurses
of Co. Meath
North Eastern Health Board

611. Ms. Rena English
Co. Tipperary

612. Mr. Michael Bergin
Kilkenny

613. Ms. Christina Lambert
Co. Wexford

614. Behavioural Nurse
Psychotherapists
North Eastern Health Board's
Psychiatric Services

615. Palliative Care Team
Co. Monaghan

616. Mr. Liam Noud
Carlow

617. Ms. Margot Hanley
Limerick Regional Hospital

618. Ward Sisters
Limerick Regional Hospital

619. RNMH's
Early Childhood Services
Brothers of Charity
Co. Galway

620. Staff of Aras Attracta
Swinford
Co. Mayo

621. Staff of St. Mary's Day Hospital
Block 7
Orthopaedic Hospital
Cork

622. Ms. Rita Bourke
Galway

623. Control & Restraint Team
North Eastern Health Board

624. Ms. Agnes O'Sullivan
Co. Cork

625. National Superintendent Public
Health Management Group
Representing all Health Boards

626. Nursing Officer & Deputy
Nursing Officers
Midleton

627. Staff from Cavan Day Hospital

628. SIPTU Members of CPN Group
c/o St. Davnet's Hospital
Monaghan

629. Mr. John Cronin
Co. Cork

630. Nursing Officers & Deputy
Nursing Officers
St. Stephen's Hospital
Co. Cork

631. National Nursing Council
SIPTU

632. Area Public Health Nurses
Western Health Board

633. Ms. Myra Sherry
Co. Kildare

634. Ms. Evelyn Conran
Dublin 14

635. Ms. Anne Moynihan
Co. Limerick

636. Ms. Bernadette Gannon
Galway

637. Nurse Teachers Group in the
Services of People with
Mental Handicap

638. Ms. Anne Cardiff
Wexford General Hospital

639. Midwives
Erinville Maternity Hospital
Cork

640. Ms. Patricia Mearley
Dublin 18

641. Outpatient Department
James Connolly Memorial Hospital
Dublin 15

642. Carlow/Kilkenny Home Care Team
St. Luke's Hospital
Kilkenny

643. Ms. Anne-Marie Lanigan
South Eastern Health Board

644. Nurses from
James Connolly Memorial Hospital
Dublin 15

645. Nursing Officer Group

646. Ms. Eithna Gaffney
& Ms. Eileen Moylan
Dublin 6W

647. Ms. Noreen Delaney
Co. Tipperary

648. Ms. Siobhan Carroll O'Brien
Co. Cork

649. Ms. Mary McMahon
Limerick Regional Hospital

650. Ms. Margaret Lally
Limerick Regional Hospital

651. Ms. Pauline Kilcoyne
Limerick Regional Hospital

652. Ms. Mary Keary
Co. Galway

653. Nursing Officers & Deputy
Nursing Officers
Louth/Meath Mental Health
Services

654. Ms. Christina Hickey
Kilkenny

655. NCHD Committee
Irish Medical Organisation

656. Ms. Rosaleen Crawley Clare
Co. Louth

657. Ms. Eithne Cusack
Dublin 15

658. Ms. Olga Price

659. Mr. Paddy Hyde
Southern Health Board

660. Ms. Nuala Rafferty
Co. Meath

661. Ms. Helen O'Connor
Co. Kerry

662. Senior Staff Nurses
Renal Unit
Beaumont Hospital

663. Domiciliary Midwives

664. Ms. Rose McLoughlin
Dublin 4

665. J.C.M. Unit
James Connolly Special Children's
Hospital
Carndonagh

666. Lecturers
Department of Nursing
University College Cork

667. An Bord Altranais

668. Registered Nurses
College of Commerce
Cork

669. Irish Nurses Organisation

670. Ms. Kay Coburn
Carlow

671. Group of Nurses
Forensic Services
Central Mental Hospital

672. Mr. Seamus O'Mahony
Co. Dublin

673. Nurse Managers
Letterkenny General Hospital

674. Anonymous

675. Clonmel Branch of the
Psychiatric Nurses Association

676. Temporary Nurses
North Eastern Health Board

677. P Madden
Southern Health Board

678. Public Health Nurses
Ballinasloe

679. Ms. Mary Byrne
North Eastern Health Board

680. Ms. Noreen Lyons
Co. Kerry

681. Dr. J Bernard Walsh
Dublin 8

682. Quality Assurance in Nursing
Association

683. SIPTU Forensic Psychiatric
Nurses
Central Mental Hospital

684. Ms. Bernadette McGough
Co. Monaghan

685. M H Gilmartin
University College Hospital Cork

686. Ms. Kathleen Harrington
Co. Tipperary

687. Nurses within the Nursing Alliance

688. Ms. Maura Tummon
Galway

689. Irish Public Health Nurses
Nationwide

690. Mr. Thomas Keary
Co. Galway

691. Mr. John Shannon

692. The Western Branch
Institute of Community
Health Nursing

693. Anonymous

694. Mr. Patrick J McDermott
Co. Roscommon

695. Chief Executive Officers
from the Health Boards

696. C.A. MacGregor
Co. Louth

697. Ms. Rosaleen Murnane
Dublin 7

698. The Blood Transfusion
Service Board

699. Community Psychiatric Nurses
Longford/Westmeath Catchment
Area
Midland Health Board

700. IMPACT
The Public Sector Trade

701. Psychiatric Nurses Association

702. The Adelaide Hospital Society

703. The Nurse Tutors and
Clinical Teachers Section of the
Irish Nurses' Organisation

704. Monaghan Branch of the
Psychiatric Nurses Association